The
Astrology
Journal

✳

A CELESTIAL GUIDE TO RECORDING YOUR
Cosmic Journey

Mecca Woods

ADAMS MEDIA

NEW YORK LONDON TORONTO SYDNEY NEW DELHI

Adams Media
An Imprint of Simon & Schuster, Inc.
100 Technology Center Drive
Stoughton, Massachusetts 02072

First Adams Media hardcover edition August 2021

ADAMS MEDIA and colophon are trademarks of Simon & Schuster.

For information about special discounts for bulk purchases, please contact Simon & Schuster Special Sales at 1-866-506-1949 or business@simonandschuster.com.

The Simon & Schuster Speakers Bureau can bring authors to your live event. For more information or to book an event contact the Simon & Schuster Speakers Bureau at 1-866-248-3049 or visit our website at www.simonspeakers.com.

Interior design by Julia Jacintho
Illustrations by Emma Taylor

Manufactured in the United States of America

1 2021

ISBN 978-1-5072-1654-5

Contains material adapted from the following titles published by Adams Media, an Imprint of Simon & Schuster, Inc.: *Astrology for Happiness and Success* by Mecca Woods, copyright © 2018, ISBN 978-1-5072-0782-6; *The Mixology of Astrology* by Aliza Kelly Faragher, copyright © 2018, ISBN 978-1-5072-0815-1; *Moon Magic* by Diane Ahlquist, copyright © 2017 by Diane Ahlquist, ISBN 978-1-5072-0501-3; *How to Be an Astrologer* by Constance Stellas, copyright © 2020, ISBN 978-1-5072-1301-8; and *The Green Witch's Grimoire* by Arin Murphy-Hiscock, copyright © 2020, ISBN 978-1-5072-1354-4.

Contents

Introduction...6

PART ONE
Getting Started—8

Chapter One: Astrology Basics.................................10

Sun Signs and Their Elements and Qualities...................................11

The Elements (Triplicities) 11
The Qualities (Quadruplicities)......................................12
Aries: March 21-April 19..13
Taurus: April 20-May 20..14
Gemini: May 21-June 20..14
Cancer: June 21-July 22..15
Leo: July 23-August 22..16
Virgo: August 23-September 22......................................17
Libra: September 23-October 22....................................18
Scorpio: October 23-November 21 18
Sagittarius: November 22-December 21...........................19
Capricorn: December 22-January 19..............................20
Aquarius: January 20-February 18.................................21
Pisces: February 19-March 20 22

The Moon and Its Impact on Your Life..23
   The Moon's Phases 23
      The New Moon 23
      The Full Moon 24
      The Waning Moon 24
      The Dark Moon 24
   The Void-of-Course Moon 25

The Sun and Its Impact on Your Life...26
   The Seasonal Solar Cycle 26

Eclipses and Their Impact on Your Life 27

The Planets and Their Impact on Your Life..............................28
   Mercury Retrograde...29
      What Does Mercury Retrograde Mean? 29
      How to Approach Life When Mercury Is Retrograde......30
      Special Note for Geminis and Virgos............................ 30
   Venus Retrograde 31
   Mars Retrograde 31
   Saturn Return 31
      What Does the Saturn Return Mean? 32
      How to Handle Life During a Saturn Return 33
   Jupiter Transits 33
   Uranus, Neptune, and Pluto Transits 34

Moving Forward 35

Chapter Two: Using Your Journal 36

What Is an Astrological Journal?..37

The Benefits of Keeping an Astrological Journal 37

Tips for Productive Journaling..39

How to Fill In This Journal..40
   Record...40
      That Day's Key Information 40

Using Your Birth Chart to Learn More 40

Your Horoscope 40

Your Mood 41

Reflect 41

PART TWO

The Journal—42

Resources 186

Index 188

Introduction

Astrologers are well known for their forecasts and predictions, so it is easy to think that the practice of astrology is about focusing solely on the future. While it's true that astrology does help us prepare and plan for the future, astrologers—and you!—can also look at the past and the present moment to answer life's questions, big and small. Do full moons often leave you feeling energized and restless? Is today's horoscope offering key insights into your self-development? When is the best time to launch your new business venture?

The answers to these questions and more can be found in the stars. Astrology is the study of cycles: planetary and seasonal cycles. Given enough time, as these cycles repeat, patterns are formed. Tracking and documenting these patterns in this journal will help you make astrological predictions and answer questions about yourself and your life. The process is similar to what economists do when predicting financial trends or what historians do when showing us how certain events or movements have brought us to where we are today. You can apply these same principles of reflection and forecasting in your own life. In order to ready yourself for the future, you'll need a good grasp on where you currently are and what's brought you to this moment. This journal provides a space to reflect on your own journey using your birth chart as your map and the stars as your guide.

Whether you're new to astrology or are an astrology enthusiast, you can tailor this book to your own life experiences. Just as your birth chart is uniquely tailored to you as an individual, this journal should be too. If you are very interested in moon phases, make those observations a big part of your daily reflection. If your horoscope helps guide your daily decisions, let their themes take center stage. Use the prompts to encourage self-reflection on the past and open your mind to new possibilities for the future. If you need a little help on how or where to get started, the information in Part 1 of this book will give you a strong foundation. With time, you might even find your astrological knowledge expanding as you grow through your experiences too.

Keeping track of how the patterns of the planets affect and align with your own patterns can help you with decision-making, and can help you become more firmly rooted within yourself. As you're moving along on your path, you'll never really lose yourself or your way because you have a strong sense of self, thanks to the observations and patterns you've recorded. When you find yourself faced with obstacles or difficult questions, the thoughts, feelings, reflections, and insights that you've written in this journal will help you overcome those challenges. Let *The Astrology Journal* ground you, inform you, and inspire you!

PART ONE
Getting Started

For as long as astrology has been around (more than two thousand years, to be exact!), astrologers have used it as a tool to help bring about a desired result or outcome using both cosmic timing and the power of the stars that a person is born under—a.k.a. their sun sign. Fast-forward to today, and we find the field of astrology being used for all sorts of things, from picking the perfect date to picking the perfect outfit. Astrology can help you better identify your special qualities and teach you how to marry them with auspicious timing to find the things in life that you're searching for. And if astrology can help you with the smaller stuff, why wouldn't you use its power to help you find the happiness and success that you're *really* looking for?

Part 1 of *The Astrology Journal* will teach you the basics of astrology and journaling to get you off on the right foot. Chapter 1 covers information about each sun sign; its elements and qualities; and key movements and alignments of the sun, moon, and planets that can impact your life. Once you've learned that foundation, Chapter 2 will show you exactly how to use this journal. You'll learn the many benefits of keeping an astrological journal, along with tips for filling out each blank page and making your journaling practice productive. Let's get started.

CHAPTER ONE
Astrology Basics

You don't have to be an expert in astrology to get the most out of this journal, but the background information in this chapter will help you understand the cycles, events, and influences that can impact your life. You will discover a summary of your sun sign's tendencies, including layers like elements and qualities.

Next, we'll move on to understanding how other celestial bodies affect life on Earth. From moon phases to eclipses and from Mercury retrograde to Saturn returns, you'll get insight on how these key events might influence your mood, decisions, and day-to-day life.

Sun Signs and Their Elements and Qualities

The most important thing when it comes to understanding your astrological sign is the placement of the sun at your birth—specifically, which of the twelve zodiac signs the sun was in when you were born. The placement of this vivid star reveals your sun sign, which is usually what magazine and online horoscopes focus on. The astrological year begins with Aries the ram and concludes with Pisces the fish. The sun sign reflects your main personality traits and preferences, as well as the "imperfections" in your character.

Each sign, in addition to having its own nature, is ruled by a planet (Venus, Mars, and so on), an element (air, water, fire, or earth), and a quality (cardinal, fixed, or mutable). Let's take a look at the elements and qualities before we learn more about each astrological sun sign.

THE ELEMENTS (TRIPLICITIES)

The elements are the building blocks of nature. Each element has three astrological signs associated with it:

- Aries, Leo, and Sagittarius form the fire triplicity.
- Taurus, Virgo, and Capricorn form the earth triplicity.
- Gemini, Libra, and Aquarius form the air triplicity.
- Cancer, Scorpio, and Pisces constitute the water triplicity.

These elements can help you understand some of the foundational nature of each astrological sign.

- **Earth:** Earth signs are associated with practicality and conservation. The element of earth represents stability, abundance, physical well-being, patience, strength, and production. The earth provides humans with food and shelter thanks to that abundance and production.

- **Air:** Air signs are associated with communication and the intellect. After all, wind carries pollen and seeds, enabling growth and nature to spread, much like the human mind germinates words and ideas that can spark development and discussions within others. The element of air represents curiosity, openness, wit, socializing, rationality, and objectivity.

- **Fire:** Fire signs are generally energetic and inspirational. The element of fire is associated with action, independence, passion, confidence, enthusiasm, and creativity. Fire symbolizes the will to live and the life force that courses through every single living creature on the planet.

- **Water:** Water signs are considered emotional and nurturing. Water is associated with healing, caring, feelings, intuition, cleansing, consecration, and connecting with your deep psyche. As with air, you cannot live without water. Water is often thought of as a calm energy, but it can also rage like a hurricane or a tsunami. In this way, water reflects the wide range of human emotion. Water sources were often considered holy places; springs and wells were locations where you could speak to deities or nature spirits.

THE QUALITIES (QUADRUPLICITIES)

Each astrological sun sign is also associated with a quality: cardinal, fixed, or mutable.

- The beginnings of spring, summer, fall, and winter describe the cardinal nature of Aries, Cancer, Libra, and Capricorn. These signs are excellent at taking action and starting new initiatives, but may be a bit too bossy or domineering in their pursuits.

- The months when each season is well established characterize the fixed signs: Taurus, Leo, Scorpio, and Aquarius. These signs are consistent, steady forces that maintain movement, but have a tendency to be stubborn or rigid in their convictions.

- The months in which the seasons change characterize the mutable signs: Gemini, Virgo, Sagittarius, and Pisces. These signs welcome growth through their adaptable spirits, but can also fear commitment and lack reliability.

Let's look more in depth at each of the twelve sun signs.

ARIES: MARCH 21–APRIL 19

Known as the firstborn of the zodiac and a fire sign, you're a true pioneer and innovator. Because of the sheer determination and the fire that you carry in your heart, there's hardly anything that can stop you from going after something (or someone) you want. One reason for this is because your zodiac sign is ruled by Mars, the planet associated with the Roman god of war. With your warrior spirit, you're able to conquer challenges set before you, all the while venturing out into new territories and experiences without any of the fears or reservations that may slow others down.

While some may criticize your approach as reckless and impulsive, at your core you have a deep-seated need to express yourself as authentically and sincerely as possible. In fact, originality is one of your superpowers—as is your way of bluntly telling it like it is. All the natural, unbridled power that you possess can make it easy to burn yourself out when you allow the fear of losing or appearing weak to get the best of you. As the zodiac sign linked with the fearless god who wins at all costs and never backs down from a fight, it's important for you to recognize that not everything you do has to be a battle or a win-lose scenario.

Acknowledging this takes self-awareness, and part of this awareness means having the ability to make room for others to win—recognizing that their winning doesn't mean that you lose. When passion and creativity are your source of motivation, you give yourself the freedom to truly *be* yourself.

Taurus: APRIL 20-MAY 20

Sensual. Grounded. Determined. These are just some of the words used to describe the earthy, palpable mojo that you were born with. As a zodiac sign associated with the element of earth, much of your focus is rooted in the material world, where you strive to achieve and maintain stability and financial security. You're largely concerned with building things that last, from relationships to a career. You need to be sure that what you're investing in is worth your time and energy; you'll barely lift a finger if you know something or someone isn't worth it. Though once you are invested, you're loyal to a fault.

Being ruled by Venus, the mythological goddess of love, beauty, and pleasure, the physical body is also your playground. While you can go between dressing up and dressing down (depending on your level of comfort), you never miss the chance to adorn yourself with high-end baubles and fabrics.

Some of your biggest challenges center on an inability to let go and adapt to change. This can lead to staying in situations well past their prime, due to a fear of uncertainty or complacency. While you can be a trailblazer, unafraid to rock the boat when it comes to pursuing something you believe in or maintaining your principles, you can also risk losing some of that moxie if you feel like you might lose your security.

Gemini: MAY 21-JUNE 20

As the zodiac sign associated with intellect and the art of communication, you thrive on thoughts, words, and education—learning as much as you can, whenever you can. Always with a funny anecdote or an interesting tidbit of information at the ready, you can often be found holding court over a crowd of people, entertaining them for hours on end with your wit. Associated with the element of air, you tend to need space (and lots of it) to come and go as you please. Even if you choose to settle down, you need a schedule (and an understanding partner) that enables you to stay on the move, picking up new experiences and knowledge as you go.

You identify most with all things trendy, fresh, and cutting-edge, often quick to lose interest in anything more than five minutes old. While this makes you an incredibly innovative, razor-sharp thinker, you must also be able to guard against boredom, overstimulation, and distraction. In a world that moves at hyperspeed, you have no trouble keeping up. It's the slowing down that throws you off. This extends to feelings too: When your mind is always busy processing every thought and emotion that filters through it, it becomes hard to find the time or space to thoroughly and honestly feel what you feel.

Being a sign of duality means that you have a gift for finding the common thread between abstract, conflicting, or unrelated ideas. You also have a knack for juggling multiple projects, interests, and social circles in a way that would make another person's head spin. This gift enables you to keep room in your life, in your head, or in your conversations for many things (and many people) at once. The challenge here, though, is to avoid spreading yourself too thin with too many interests, activities, or casual acquaintances.

CANCER: JUNE 21-JULY 22

In many ways, the Moon represents the heart: holding memories, feelings, and deep, soul-felt connections to others. As the sign associated with the Moon, you, too, are like a heart. Prioritizing relationships with others, you can be found at the center of a community or family (much like a heartbeat), running the show with your own brand of strength, support, and tender care.

Defined by the element of water, you live in the realm of feelings and intuition. You possess the power to plug in to the pulse of the collective, moving souls and setting trends with your emotional honesty, genuine compassion for others, and old-soul wisdom. While you may get pegged as being overly moody, your many moods are really your way of assessing a person, situation, or experience and adjusting accordingly to match your surroundings—kind of like a chameleon. Your feelings act as your guideposts, helping you react to situations accordingly, whether it's through kindness and nurture or through your tough, protective shell.

Once you do let your guard down for someone, you remain loyal and loving to them. This is a big reason why you are celebrated for your nurturing spirit: When you give to your family and community, you give with very few limits. However, as a sign motivated by emotional security, it is incredibly hurtful for you when you feel that the loyalty and kindness you show others isn't reciprocated. You must learn how to be okay with putting yourself and your needs first at times (sans guilt), as well as how to develop a sense of self that exists outside of the identity of your clan.

LEO: JULY 23-AUGUST 22

As the astrological sign ruled by the brightest, hottest star in our solar system (the Sun), you bring that megawatt power down to Earth with your warmth, generosity, incomparable talent, and killer style. Essentially, you were born to stand out. This is because, at your core, you have a desire to express yourself in all your fabulousness—unabashed and unfiltered. In fact, this authentic self-expression is often your driving force. When you show up as you are, you fuel and inspire the rest of us by shining your light with a ferocity and verve that can only warrant the deepest appreciation. You also thrive on that appreciation, seeking out life experiences and everyday connections with others that thrust you into the spotlight to be celebrated and adored.

As a natural-born leader, you gain followers with your fiery spirit, unwavering loyalty, and creative genius. However, when you lose sight of your own specialness by seeing yourself through another's eyes instead of your own, it can dull your shine. For example, when you find yourself doing things solely for attention or applause, it's time to take a step back and remember how unique you are outside of the gaze of an audience. As a sign that is all about self-expression, you need to live from a self-centered place. No, not in the obnoxious, inconsiderate sense of the word, but in the sense of doing things that make you happy regardless of whether people are watching. When you are focusing on being the best you—for yourself—you attract the kind of good vibes that will make you truly successful in things like love and family relationships.

VIRGO: AUGUST 23-SEPTEMBER 22

As a Virgo, you are known for efficiency, productivity, and finding solutions to the toughest problems, so you always get the job done right. Sharing a planetary ruler (Mercury) with Gemini, you are also blessed with the same sharp mind and ability to think on your feet. Mercury bestows you with the power to break down and process information at lightning speed. As an earth sign, you take things a step further by focusing on how ideas and information can be skillfully applied to the real world.

You pride yourself on being useful, and this is one of the things that drives you to help others. This is why you may find yourself in a profession that involves helping others, such as coaching or medicine. Represented in astrology by virginity and purity (a.k.a. the virgin), a Virgo's life mission is to make things better through a process of refinement. Whether it's through fitness and nutrition or by creating the patent for the next life-changing invention, your passion is to show the rest of us what needs improving and how to improve it.

Still, it's important that you are careful not to define your identity solely by how much you do (or don't do). Being your own toughest critic, you tend to push yourself harder and further than most, setting exceptionally high expectations and blaming yourself when things don't go as perfectly as you planned. You must learn to master the art of surrender and acceptance. While being practical and prepared is a good thing, so is having faith that things will work out as they should and (even more so) having faith in yourself.

In your relationships, you thrive on helping others and being needed. As a Virgo, your mission is to develop your powers of discernment to figure out who (and what) deserves your attention and who (and what) doesn't.

LIBRA: SEPTEMBER 23-OCTOBER 22

With your planetary ruler, Venus, and your natural element of air, you are interested in building social capital and bridges between people, creating a pleasant atmosphere, and inspiring artistic expression. As someone inherently dedicated to fairness and justice, you strive to keep the peace between yourself and those around you, which is why you are known for diplomacy and sharp negotiating skills. Thanks to your keen eye for all things pretty and your love for tranquility, you always know what to say, wear, or do to elevate a room, experience, or relationship.

As adept as you are at creating and holding space for others, a big part of your growth and fulfillment centers around learning how to establish relationships with others that are reciprocal and balanced. This learning process may also mean setting healthy boundaries.

Oftentimes, people misinterpret you as disingenuous because of your ability to understand and validate both sides of an argument and your extremely affable personality. What people don't understand is that this behavior is actually a result of fear: the fear of ruffling feathers by picking sides in a way that may alienate others or yourself. You must learn how to hold space for yourself, recognizing that your identity is not defined by your relationship to others but rather your relationship to yourself. Getting back to who you are will allow you to bring all your wonderful and unique gifts to every aspect of your life, including love.

SCORPIO: OCTOBER 23-NOVEMBER 21

Scorpios are often the most misunderstood sign in astrology. This is because of the themes that Scorpio is associated with: death, rebirth, and transformation—all of which are avoided in society, as they are considered either too heavy, uncomfortable, or inappropriate to tackle head-on. Not for you, though. You're always ready to dive into them headfirst, taking whoever is brave enough along for the ride with you.

Not one to skim the surface, you thrive on emotional depth and exploring the subconscious and its themes. Not only do you have the keen insight into human behavior that gives you the ability to spot people and their motivations a mile away; you also have a mystery and magnetism about you that both pushes people away and attracts them to you. You are looking for a sense of wholeness within yourself and with a partner by way of absolute intimacy and unfiltered emotional honesty. Co-ruled by passionate Mars and fearless Pluto, you are turned on by the messy, mysterious sides of the human experience.

For all your strength, you are also incredibly sensitive. This sensitivity is one of the gifts that makes you a deeply devoted and loving partner and friend. However, when that sensitivity is triggered by your insecurities, you struggle with holding grudges. Being co-ruled by the two planets related to anger, power, and traumatic experiences, you don't take your feelings lightly. Overall, your lesson is to learn how to love yourself with the same ferocity that you would a soul mate.

SAGITTARIUS: NOVEMBER 22–DECEMBER 21

The jet-setter and the shaman. The intellectual and the goofball. There's a reason why your zodiac sign is linked to a creature that is half human and half beast; it's this duality that makes you both the wandering child and the wise old soul. This is also why people turn to you for sage advice, entertaining stories, and thought-provoking conversation. Ruled by the planet Jupiter, also known as the king of the gods in Roman mythology, your lifelong quest is to help the rest of us answer the big questions about life and our roles in it. This is why your sign is considered the teacher as well as the student. Represented by the warm, dynamic element of fire, and ruled by the planet associated with indulgence and abundance, you have a lighthearted nature that allows you to find the silver lining in just about any situation.

For all your enthusiasm and energy, problems emerge when you feel that your freedom is being threatened. This is when the more primal side of you appears, as you are ready to take off at a moment's notice,

dropping your commitments rather than taking on the responsibility that lies before you. An idealist at heart, you can become so caught up in the promise of a dream come true that you overlook the need to buckle down to actually turn that dream into something real. This results in numerous false starts and unfinished projects. In your relationships, this can also lead you to miss crucial red flags or seem noncommittal.

CAPRICORN: DECEMBER 22-JANUARY 19

Reserved and meticulous, you don't expend your energy on anyone or anything unless you know it's worth it. Ruled by Saturn, the planet linked to responsibility, rules, and achievement, you approach the world with a no-nonsense strategy and a realistic outlook. For you, time is money, and you don't like wasting either. However, you are always ready and willing to offer friends and family a helping hand, even at a moment's notice. Whether you're providing someone with financial advice or lending your time and skills to aid a friend in need, when folks call on you, you are ready to help.

You teach the rest of us how to turn our ideas and passions into something tangible, like a well-funded money market account. As the zodiac sign connected to status, awards, and recognition, you have no trouble with putting in the long, painstaking hours to sharpen your skills and get ahead. Your dedication to success is what makes you both envied and admired among your peers. For you, it's work first, rewards later.

However, things start to get a bit sticky when your preoccupation with rules and responsibility prevents you from being open to change or able to go with the flow. Although your ability to keep things in check is one of your gifts, you can paralyze yourself with a fear of losing your security, bringing out the control freak in you. Ultimately, one of the biggest lessons you must learn is how to operate from a place of security from within—to stay centered and grounded in an ever-changing world. Your goal is to establish your own internal compass that supports the courage and peace of mind that comes from being true to yourself and your values—no matter your salary. This compass will also guide you through other aspects of your life, including love.

AQUARIUS: JANUARY 20-FEBRUARY 18

Ruled by Saturn, you have a fixation on the rules, tearing them down in favor of a better system—especially when the preexisting rules only benefit a small fraction of society. This is where your secondary ruler, Uranus, comes in. In astrology, it is Uranus's job to break the rules and societal norms. It's not uncommon to see Aquarians dedicate their lives (and at times, sacrifice their safety) to create a better world. Some Aquarians do this through the avenues of tech and science, as well as activism, community organizing, or public administration.

As an air sign, not a moment goes by that you aren't coming up with your next idea. Your sharp intellect makes you and others born under your sign some of the most innovative thinkers around. Thanks to your genuine care for others, many of your ideas are geared toward supporting the collective. Your mission is to teach the rest of the world how to work together as a community while still making room for one another's individuality.

A major theme in your life is honoring your individuality regardless of how unaccepting others may be. When imbalanced, you might struggle with either people-pleasing at the expense of your own needs, or becoming so nonconformist that you alienate yourself from others. Essentially, your biggest lesson is learning how to express yourself in a way that honors your individuality without trampling on the individuality of others. One way to do this is by recognizing that your beliefs aren't necessarily the correct or only beliefs. Honoring your individuality will go a long way in helping you succeed in all aspects of your life, including love.

PISCES: FEBRUARY 19-MARCH 20

As a water sign, you are most concerned with emotional and spiritual healing, including bridging the gap between the emotional and spiritual realms. During this quest, you teach the rest of the world lessons about compassion, forgiveness, faith, and love in all forms.

While many people peg you as being soft and easily pushed over, the fact of the matter is that while the rest of the world hides from their wounds and tries to cover up their vulnerability, you courageously love and accept others, despite the risk of being hurt. You can see and feel another's suffering while providing exactly what they need to heal. Meanwhile, your natural sweet charm has you raking in the admirers with little effort.

Part of staying sane means setting and maintaining boundaries. Without healthy boundaries, you are vulnerable to giving too much of yourself or absorbing too much (specifically negative emotions) from others. Either way, you are left feeling drained in your mind, body, and soul. Ultimately, what you must guard against is sacrificing yourself and your happiness on behalf of the needs of others. This skill will translate to many parts of your life, including family relationships and love.

The Moon and Its Impact on Your Life

The moon spends approximately two and a half days in each zodiac sign and takes approximately twenty-nine days to complete her journey through the zodiac. To simplify the use of the moon in your astrological planning, just note the sign the moon is in, and concentrate on activities that correlate with the nature of that sign. For example, host a party when the moon is in Libra. Consider volunteer work or dealing with your pets when the moon is in Virgo or Pisces. When the moon is in Taurus, it's a good time to look for a house, buy furniture, or cook a good meal. Since the moon is the celestial light that governs our emotions and highlights what we need to feel safe, supported, and loved, consider making note of how you feel as the moon filters through each sign. You should also do this as the moon goes through each phase of the lunar cycle, and note how you feel during other key lunar events.

The Moon's Phases

The lunar cycle begins with the waxing phase—that is the time from the new moon until the full moon. The waning phase commences after the full moon and is called the third quarter moon; it concludes with the dark of the moon. The general rule is that when you want to attract or grow something in your life, do it in the first half of the lunar month, when the moon appears to be increasing in the sky. Banishing, or anything associated with decrease or reduction (such as kicking a bad habit), should be performed in the second half of the cycle, when the moon appears to shrink away in the sky.

The New Moon

Noted on most calendars, the new moon is the time when energy is increasing, making it the time to initiate new projects. Each month's new moon is in the same sign as that month's sun sign, and the full moon is in the opposite sign. There is a feeling of renewal with each new moon.

This is the time to start looking for a new job, begin a new wellness plan, initiate a project, or plan a relocation or a trip. When you plan around the lunar phases, you are synchronized with the natural flow of energy. If you begin a project during the new moon and stick with it, you should see some results of your work at the full moon. This is approximately two weeks. This is the sowing phase, and you are planting seeds for the future.

The Full Moon

Everyone feels intense energy at this time. Cancerians, in particular, may need to let off some steam. No matter where your sun or moon may be, you may feel more vibrant than usual, very moody, or restless. Contact with water is restorative during the full moon. It is a good time to find ways to ground and soothe yourself, as feelings that may be over-whelming or upsetting could come bubbling up to the surface. Full moons can be times for celebration too, as the air is buzzing with excitement and seeds that were sown at the new moon may reach fulfillment at this time.

The Waning Moon

Right after the full moon, you may notice that things become a little slower and you may feel as if nothing is happening. This is a time to keep up your actions and finish up the projects begun at the previous new moon. Some projects, of course, take a good deal longer than a single lunar cycle. When the moon is waning, give yourself some downtime and don't go full tilt. A little relaxation and fun is the best medicine during the waning moon.

The Dark Moon

The last three days of the lunar cycle can feel dull, and you may be more tired than usual. This is a time to rest. That doesn't necessarily mean stay in bed, but relax—and if you do need sleep, try to get as much as you can. Pay attention to your dreams and be as inwardly oriented as your nature allows. After all, what you are doing is preparing for the next new moon, which comes soon enough.

THE VOID-OF-COURSE MOON

The term *void-of-course* (also written as the v/c or VoC moon) relates to a period of time when the moon is changing from one sign to the next, and is not connected in a major applying aspect to any other planet. When the moon is unconnected to other planets, a person can feel unmoored or confused.

The VoC moon period is a time to take a break and connect with your center. This is a time to postpone decisions and wait until the moon officially moves into the next sign before initiating anything important. When the moon is void, we're usually not able to see or discern the situation or information presented clearly. However, the VoC moon can be ideal for doing things that you don't want to see pan out or follow through. For example, use the VoC moon to schedule a meeting or discussion that you would rather not have.

During the VoC period, scale down your activities, relax, review your plans for the immediate future, and tie up loose ends and unfinished business. If you don't feel comfortable doing something when the moon is VoC, do it later. Sometimes you might not have the luxury of doing what you feel like doing, but knowing that you may be swimming upstream helps you have patience with yourself and fosters a certain benign detachment from the multitude of events and influences swirling around you.

The Sun and Its Impact on Your Life

The moon isn't the only celestial body that impacts your life, of course. The sun's life-giving rays not only provide light and warmth on a daily basis; they also inform the four seasons, the annual cycle on which Western astrology is founded.

The Seasonal Solar Cycle

The sun governs the seasons. The winter sun possesses a different energy than the summer sun, for example; it appears to be in a different place in the sky and at a different angle. The earth's axial tilt means that as we orbit, the surface of the earth moves closer to and farther away from the sun, which results in a temperature shift that varies through the seasonal cycle. Like with the moon cycle, there is a waxing and waning pattern.

- **Winter** energies are quiet, slow energies. It is a time of hibernation, of recouping energy after exhaustion.
- **Spring** energies are creative and full of potential; they are about planting seeds for future harvesting.
- **Summer** energies are expansive, lush, and robust.
- **Fall** energies are about harvesting the abundance we've created, and winding down in preparation for rest.

As you fill in this journal, keep the seasons in mind, and see if you notice any patterns between them and your life.

Eclipses and Their Impact on Your Life

Eclipses are astronomical events that occur when one celestial body moves into the shadow of another and is partially or totally shaded. Eclipses happen every year and always happen in pairs (e.g., a solar eclipse and lunar eclipse happen as part of the same process). Eclipses also repeat in cycles every eighteen years and every nine years. They are not visible in all parts of the world, but they are always potent indicators of influences and events. The most convenient way to find out when the next eclipse is in your part of the world is to look in an astrological calendar or app.

From our perspective on Earth, we experience two types of eclipses: eclipses of the sun and eclipses of the moon. These occur when the sun, earth, and moon arrange themselves in a straight or near-straight line. When the new moon's shadow crosses Earth's surface, we experience a solar eclipse, whereas when the full moon moves into the shadow of Earth, a lunar eclipse occurs. Within the spectrum of solar and lunar eclipses there are annular and penumbral eclipses. A penumbral lunar eclipse is basically a shadow cast on the moon by Earth and is significantly less dramatic than an annular solar eclipse. Annular eclipses are similar to total eclipses in that the moon precisely lines up with the sun. However, in this eclipse, the moon is at the point farthest from the earth (called apogee) and is too far away to completely block all light. Thus, the moon appears too small in the sky to cover the solar disk entirely. Annular eclipses are considered as powerful as other eclipses, with effects lasting for up to six months.

From an astrological standpoint, eclipses trigger or coincide with major life events, like getting married or divorced, getting a job or quitting one, relocating to a new home, starting a family, going back to school, dealing with illness, and more. Because eclipses are agents of change, events that happen around an eclipse often feel like a moment of crisis. The reason for this is that eclipses shake us out of stagnation and thrust us into a new phase of life. Even if we feel taken by surprise with the changes an eclipse can trigger, somewhere deep down, we find ourselves craving it.

Ultimately, it is important to remember that eclipses push us toward new heights in our personal development and growth. Oftentimes, whatever gets "eclipsed" out of our lives due to an eclipse was ready to go—and now we can move forward unfettered. Perhaps the best way to work with the eclipses is to be open to change and trust that what's happening is for your success. Another way to work with eclipses is by getting the extra rest and care your mind and body needs, as eclipses can trigger more mental and physical stress than usual.

The Planets and Their Impact on Your Life

Astrology is the art of studying planetary cycles and positions, and uses those cycles as both a language and a tool to inform the events in our lives on Earth. In the same way that you feel differently when spending time with different people, planetary motion affects you in varied ways. (As the ancient seer Hermes Trismegistus said, "As above, so below.") Studying the planetary movements and their effects upon your birth chart is perhaps the most fascinating part of astrology. Have you noticed that certain times of the year are productive and buoyant for you and other times are not? If you look at the positions of the planets in connection with your birth chart during these times, you might begin to see a pattern. You will know which times are the most beneficial and which times are the most challenging. If it is a low period for you, this might not be the time to launch a job search, build a new house, or start dating. You can capture these types of observations in the journal pages in Part 2.

Although the Internet can be a good source for daily astrological transits, it may be more convenient to have an astrological calendar. For instance, the *Daily Planetary Guide* (published annually by Llewellyn Publications) or the *We'Moon Datebook* (published annually by the We'Moon company) are great tools for keeping track of daily, weekly, and monthly astrological

events, including the lunar cycle. (You can also find information on the moon's transits on the web at https://mooncalendar.astro-seek.com or by downloading the My Moon Phase app for Android or iOS.) With these tools, you can follow the planets and determine their effects on you.

Following are some important planetary transits and events that might impact your mood, plans, or well-being. Learning more about these planetary positions will help you assess situations, make choices, and plan accordingly. By using the planets' motions, you will be able to work *with* the planets rather than *against* them. Some people hate the feeling of not being in control—if that sounds like you, being in tune with the cosmic rhythm can give you more control because you'll know just what to do and when. This is not a comprehensive list, but these are events that you should pay the most attention to as they tend to coincide with significant changes and/or experiences.

MERCURY RETROGRADE

You might have heard someone sigh, "Mercury must be retrograde" when something goes awry. This is the time when people roll their eyes in exasperation because computers and apps glitch out inexplicably, or people have to renegotiate a contract after failing to read the fine print. Appointments or events don't go as planned; people have a tendency to be late or forget the appointment entirely. In general, communications, plans, travel, and electronics go askew.

What Does Mercury Retrograde Mean?

Mercury spends about fifteen days to two months in each sign and takes a year to go through all the signs of the zodiac. When Mercury spends two months in a sign, it is because Mercury is in what's called *retrograde motion*. This happens three times in a calendar year. A retrograde planet does not physically move backward through the zodiac. When the motion of Mercury is retrograde, it is because Mercury slows in its orbit. The earth maintains its speed and seems to be overtaking

the slower-moving planet. Most planets have longer orbits than Mercury, and you will not notice their retrograde periods as often. Mercury, however, retrogrades three times a year, and you can be aware of this transit because it causes so much confusion.

How to Approach Life When Mercury Is Retrograde

Perhaps the best way to approach a Mercury retrograde is to take things down a notch and redirect your focus. Depending on the zodiac sign that Mercury is stationed in while retrograde—like Cancer or Pisces, for example—it can be a time to suspend thoughts and, instead, operate on your intuition.

Specifically, you can expect to redo, rearrange, recommit, rework, and review plans and activities during this time. You may go back to a project that you had abandoned. You may want to review plans. If traveling, be prepared for delays. Practical precautions include labeling luggage so you don't lose it, or leaving a margin of time for any retrograde shenanigans, such as a massive traffic jam or a computer foul-up with your reservations. You might also want to hold off on buying expensive tech or electronic equipment unless you've done thorough research on the product and don't mind spending a little extra on insurance or a protection plan.

Special Note for Geminis and Virgos

The two signs most personally affected by a retrograde Mercury are Gemini and Virgo, because Mercury is their ruling planet. During the retrograde periods, they may feel more discombobulated than other signs. These retrograde periods offer an opportunity for revisions, reassessments, and, most importantly, rest, which will help in every area of life. Geminis and Virgos have such active minds that taking time to slow down and reflect will help them avoid getting overwhelmed. For Geminis, this is the time to refocus their attention and minimize distractions or avoid spreading themselves too thin; for Virgos, it's a good time to go with the flow and be present in the moment rather than being hyperfocused on outcomes or things beyond their control.

Overall, the best approach is to use these periods to be more mindful with your words and actions. If feeling overworked or stressed, these three-week periods can be a great time to take a break or regroup.

Venus Retrograde

Venus only goes retrograde every eighteen months, but when it does, relationships, values, and finances tend to be in flux for that forty-day period. Progress might halt or regress, and communication can get muddled, especially in personal and professional relationships. This is a good time to re-evaluate your values and your connections to others. If feeling unfulfilled, unloved, or unappreciated, this is a good time to slow down and investigate why. For those that might struggle with feelings of insecurity or giving more than you get from others, Venus retrograde will push you to work on your self-worth.

Mars Retrograde

A Mars retrograde only happens every two years, but when the planet of anger and action goes backward, you notice. You might feel more sluggish or unmotivated. Past hurts might resurface and cause pain and frustration again. You could unintentionally lash out at others. Arguments might be hard to avoid. To deal with these feelings, try releasing pent-up energy through exercise; journaling or healthy venting; or taking a moment to breathe before responding or reacting to a situation. For those that find it a challenge to be confident or self-assertive, Mars retrograde will push you to work on this area.

Saturn Return

Saturn return is the first major astrological cycle that a person experiences in life. The first Saturn return occurs when a person is around 29-30 years old, but it's not uncommon to begin feeling the effects of this transit

as early as twenty-seven. The second Saturn return happens around fifty-eight years old, while the third takes place at eighty-seven. Note that you don't have to go through a Saturn return to experience a significant Saturn transit (as when Saturn is having a "conversation" with your sun, moon, or other major planets in your birth chart), but the return is one of the most important transits with this planet that you can have.

What Does the Saturn Return Mean?

Every 29.5 years, Saturn returns to the position it was in when you were born. For example, if you were born on April 23, 1988, your Saturn is in Capricorn. Saturn is stationed in a zodiac sign for about 2.5 years, but it's a planet with such a noticeable presence that it tends to make a big impact almost immediately. There are two ways that you can track a Saturn transit—by looking at how:

1. Saturn is activating your birth chart
2. Saturn is aspecting other planets in the sky (readers will be provided with info on how to find this in the Resources section of this journal)

When you experience your first Saturn return (which occurs between the ages of twenty-eight and thirty), you will definitely want to track how Saturn is affecting you. The Saturn return is the first astrological diagnostic tool you have to see if your life is on course. If you experience a great deal of disorder and change around age twenty-eight or twenty-nine, the purpose is to help you take responsibility for where you are so you can do something about it. If your Saturn return experiences are difficult, the best approach is to take an honest look at yourself or the situation and handle the issue head-on. If you've been a little too cavalier or have taken one too many shortcuts while Saturn is around, then this is a time when you'll be dealing with the consequences.

How to Handle Life During a Saturn Return

When you are undergoing a Saturn return, ask yourself these questions: "Am I where I want to be in all phases of my life? If not, what do I need to change to get there, and how can I plan that route step-by-step?" The Saturn return is not the time to daydream that one day you will miraculously find yourself with the job, partner, friends, career, and children that you want. It's not the time to be brutally hard on yourself either. The Saturn return is the time to say, "I am here, in the driver's seat, and I am ready to do the necessary work to steer my life in the direction I want it to go."

The best antidotes to the heaviness that Saturn brings (due to the extra weight of responsibility) are joy and self-care. Seek out the people and things that bring nourishment to your soul and love to your heart. This will help you feel lighter during your Saturn return or when Saturn makes tough aspects to your chart.

JUPITER TRANSITS

As the planet associated with luck and abundance, wherever Jupiter is stationed for the year, the transit tends to coincide with growth, opportunity, and good fortune, especially if Jupiter is making a significant aspect to your chart. For example, if Jupiter is transiting through your career zone for the year while also teaming up with your sun, the result could lead to more confidence, which could lead to a promotion or accolades for your work. On the flip side, Jupiter also shows where we can overdo it or have too much of a good thing. For example, you might make more money when Jupiter is around, but you'll have to make sure you don't spend too much too quickly or get carried away with the credit cards—otherwise, you could lose what you have just as quickly as you got it.

Uranus, Neptune, and Pluto Transits

As the three planets in the solar system farthest from Earth, the cycles of these planets tend to move much slower than that of the inner planets like the Sun, Moon, Mercury, Venus, or Mars. As a result, their impact on everyday life isn't always as noticeable as, say, a Mercury retrograde period, unless Uranus, Neptune, or Pluto is making a direct contact to the inner planets or key parts of your birth chart.

Since these three outer planets move so slowly and can spend up to two or three years making an aspect to a planet in your chart, their impact tends to trigger or coincide with more significant life events or long-term changes. In terms of health and well-being, it's not uncommon to experience heightened stress, fatigue, or an overall sense of heaviness when these planets are making tough aspects to your birth chart. As such, this could be a key time to ramp up your self-care regimen or better focus on your wellness.

- **Uranus** is the planet associated with the unconventional, liberation, innovation, and unpredictability. It takes eighty-four years for this planet to complete a trip through the entire zodiac, as it remains stationed within one zodiac sign at a time for a seven-year period. Significant Uranus transits often mark a period in your life when you're either looking to make sweeping changes or being pushed to make some, like leaving an unfulfilling career to pursue your calling or initiating a tough, yet overdue, divorce or breakup. For those of us that welcome and embrace change, a Uranus transit could be an exciting time to embark on a new chapter of life, while for those of us that are more security-oriented or risk-averse, it could be a more nerve-racking period. The best way to handle a Uranus transit is by being open to change and embracing the unexpected.

- **Neptune** is the planet associated with dreams, unconditional love, illusions, and your connection to the divine. Neptune takes a total of 165 years to visit the twelve signs in the zodiac, spending about fourteen years in each one. When you're undergoing a major Neptune transit,

it can be an incredibly heart-opening, creative, and keenly intuitive time. However, since Neptune can also erode boundaries and make it hard to accept reality, it can also be a time when you need to guard against being taken advantage of or painting too rosy of a picture about a situation or a person. The best way to harness Neptune's power is by seeking out things that uplift, soothe, and inspire you while making good use of the powerful intuition you've been gifted.

- **Pluto** is the planet that symbolizes power, rebirth, transformation, and loss. Pluto's cycle through the zodiac takes 248 years to complete, as it takes the planet at least thirteen years to move through a sign (and sometimes much longer, depending on its orbit). Pluto transits often mark deeply challenging moments in time that test your character. Usually, these moments involve an experience or a series of experiences in which you must confront a deep-seated fear; heal or bounce back from a profound loss; or make a drastic, now-or-never kind of change. The best way to handle or navigate a Pluto transit is by recognizing that Pluto helps you do two things:

  1. Let go of anything that's become unhealthy or stagnant.
  2. Figure out who you truly are at your core.

Moving Forward

Whew! That was a lot of information. Try not to feel overwhelmed—the more fully you immerse yourself in the astrological world, the more of this material you'll remember and the faster you'll recall key points. In the meantime, enjoy the process and be gentle with yourself as you're learning. Bring awareness to your strengths and work to improve any areas you see as challenges. Celebrate any takeaways you identify as you track your moods and reflections in the journal pages in Part 2.

CHAPTER TWO
Using Your Journal

This journal is an organic, evolving piece of art. It is a record of what's happening in the world around you, and also a reflection of your spirit. These pages will serve as a record of your work, a journal chronicling your development, a place to note down interesting bits of knowledge, a resource for information, and a collection of your learning and ongoing education. It is both an inspiration and a tool. This chapter will give you an overview of exactly how to use the blank pages in Part 2.

What Is an Astrological Journal?

An astrological journal is place to record what's going on in the celestial realm and reflect on how it affects your day-to-day life. You can keep key information like moon phases and eclipses, seasons, and planetary movements and alignments front of mind, and take a few moments to jot down some thoughts about your moods, feelings, and decisions. Over time, you might begin to see patterns. For example, are you often tired during a full moon? Feel frazzled when Mercury is retrograde? The act of observing and noting what you're doing and thinking reinforces your general awareness, both of the energy around you and your own. This awareness can bring valuable insights into your daily life.

The Benefits of Keeping an Astrological Journal

Creating a physical journal that captures your astrological journey is an act of love and reverence for yourself, for the natural world around you, and for your path. You might also notice that journaling about this topic helps you:

- **Deepen your astrology practice:** Journaling can strengthen your understanding of astrology in general, and how you develop and grow spiritually and personally.

- **Keep astrological events in mind:** Journaling gives you the opportunity to explore ideas and themes, uncover connections, and work out what issues are the most important to you in your practice. Bringing your awareness to astrological cycles and events can help you notice what's going on in your day-to-day life during those moments.

- **Relieve everyday stress through cosmic information:** Recording and reflecting can also be an excellent stress reliever by helping you work out your fears or anxieties about something. You might also find yourself better able to process events or emotions after you've written about them. Making connections between your emotions and astrology can help you better understand yourself and trust that what is happening is meant to help you live your best life.

- **Engage both sides of your brain:** When you write, you engage the analytical and logic-based side of your brain. Once the logical side has something to occupy it, the other side of the brain—the side associated with creativity, free association, and emotion—is freer to express itself and is more easily accessed. That creative side, when freed, is able to focus on spiritual breakthroughs, innovation, and emotional growth.

- **Develop mindfulness as you observe your reactions to astrological events:** Assessing and writing down your thoughts encourages mindfulness. When you are mindful, you are paying attention to the small details all around you and using all your senses to absorb them. Is the moonlight particularly vibrant? Is the summer breeze bringing back a powerful memory? When you live in the present moment and listen to your subconscious, you can gain valuable insight into why you do the things you do.

- **Release strong emotions:** Journaling is a way to release emotions that are overwhelming (anger, fear) and disturbing ideas that just won't leave you alone. Your journal can be a safe place to spill these out and track them. You might find that certain astrological cycles are a fruitful time for you to let go of past hurts, for example.

- **Uncover patterns over the long term:** Reviewing what you wrote about from time to time is as equally valuable as the writing itself, because a bit of time and distance can help you view connections that you might not have seen in the moment. Because many astrological cycles take quite a bit of time to complete, keeping a journal can help you notice how your body, mind, and spirit react to certain events.

You might find still more benefits of journaling once you get started!

Tips for Productive Journaling

A good way to begin journaling is by simply taking a few minutes at the end of the day to fill out one of the pages. Don't worry about doing it every single day; it should be a joyful experience, not a chore. Here are some tips for beginning (or think of them as refreshers if you've done this before):

- **Start with short sessions so you don't feel daunted.** Five or ten minutes can be enough to jot down ideas or feelings.

- **Treat your journaling time as self-care time.** Journal in a private, quiet place, and remember that your journal is for you alone. Create as comforting and peaceful an environment as possible.

- **Set up a routine.** Our minds usually work well with routines because they decrease the time required to get into the right headspace for the next scheduled activity. So journal at roughly the same time in the same place. This can be while you're having your morning coffee or just before bed—whenever works best for you.

- **Write quickly and don't censor yourself.** Let the ideas go where they will. The entry doesn't have to make any kind of deep statement when you reread it. Don't worry about editing yourself or making things perfect.

How to Fill In This Journal

Each page in Part 2 has two sections: Record and Reflect. Following is information about how to use each section.

Record

This is the area where you'll capture what's happening on that particular day.

That Day's Key Information

In this section, you'll mark the day, time, and any key astrological points, such as astrological and lunar cycles, retrogrades, and eclipses. Keeping track of these cycles makes you more aware of what's going on around you, both on our planet and in the heavens.

Using Your Birth Chart to Learn More

Your sun sign and the moon phases can give you a lot of insight into your personality and tendencies, but a birth chart can give you even more details that can help you round out your celestial persona. A birth chart shows where the planets were on the date, time, and place of your birth. This snapshot of the heavens at the moment of birth offers a unique method of interpreting your personality and life path. Feel free to add relevant details from your birth chart to these journal pages. Your birth chart can also be a key to understanding deep unconscious motivations and influences, and a guideline for planning for upcoming events in your life. You can obtain your birth chart for free from websites like www.astro.com or www.astro-charts.com. There's also an app called TimePassages that allows you to access and learn about your chart (the app offers a free and a paid membership).

Your Horoscope

Next, jot down a few key takeaways from your sun sign horoscope that day. For a helpful daily horoscope, check out the TimePassages app, or, of course, my daily horoscope offerings on www.bustle.com. Feel free to go with whatever daily horoscope that resonates most with you. Don't worry about capturing every word; just focus on main themes that stick out to you.

Your Mood

The Record section also includes a box in which to capture your emotions or overall mood at the beginning and end of the day. You could draw in a face, fill in the box with a color that you feel corresponds to your mood for that day, or track your mood in any other way that works for you.

REFLECT

In this section of each journal page, you can follow the prompts to jot down specific events that happened that day, key takeaways from your experiences, or astrological patterns you've noticed and how you can apply that information moving forward.

If you are struggling to find something to write about, you can also think about these questions:

- What sign was the moon in on your toughest day this month?
- What sign was the moon in on your best days this month?
- What key astrological events did you observe this month?
- Did you learn anything?
- What will you do with that information moving forward?

Over time, your journal will provide an overview of where you were spiritually, what you focused on, and how you grew and developed. The takeaways that you identify can enrich your life and improve your well-being.

PART TWO

The Journal

Your astrology practice can pique curiosity, lend reassurance, spark motivation, and help you recognize and appreciate your natural-born gifts. Fill these journal pages with your observations, and let them lead you to spiritual and personal growth. Above all, enjoy the process and have fun!

Record

Date: _____ Day of the Week: _____ Time: _____

Today's Astrology:

Lunar Cycle: ....

Astrological Season:

....

Retrogrades:

....

Eclipses:

....

Other Events:

....

....

Takeaways from Today's Horoscope:

....
....
....
....
....
....
....
....
....
....
....
....

How I Felt

Start of the Day:

End of the Day:

Reflect

Did today's horoscope come true? ◯ Yes ◯ No
◯ Partially ....
....

What happened today?

....
....
....
....
....
....
....
....
....
....
....
....
....
....

What were my key takeaways from today's experiences?

....
....
....
....
....
....
....
....
....
....
....

What key astrological events influenced today?

....
....
....
....
....
....
....
....
....
....

Other Notes for Today:

Record

Date: Day of the Week: Time:

Today's Astrology:

Lunar Cycle:..

Astrological Season:

....

Retrogrades:

....

Eclipses:

....

Other Events:

....

....

Takeaways from Today's Horoscope:

....
....
....
....
....
....
....
....
....
....
....
....

How I Felt

Start of the Day:

End of the Day:

Reflect

Did today's horoscope come true? ○ Yes ○ No
○ Partially ....
....

What happened today?
....
....
....
....
....
....
....
....
....
....
....
....
....

What were my key takeaways from today's experiences?
....
....
....
....
....
....
....
....
....
....

What key astrological events influenced today?
....
....
....
....
....
....
....
....
....
....

Other Notes for Today:

Record

Date: Day of the Week: Time:

Today's Astrology:

Lunar Cycle: ....

Astrological Season:

....

Retrogrades:

....

Eclipses:

....

Other Events:

....

....

Takeaways from Today's Horoscope:

....
....
....
....
....
....
....
....
....
....
....
....

How I Felt

Start of the Day:

End of the Day:

Reflect

Did today's horoscope come true? ○ Yes ○ No
○ Partially ....
....

What happened today?

....
....
....
....
....
....
....
....
....
....
....
....

What were my key takeaways from today's experiences?

....
....
....
....
....
....
....
....
....
....

What key astrological events influenced today?

....
....
....
....
....
....
....
....
....

Other Notes for Today:

Record

Date: Day of the Week: Time:

Today's Astrology:

Lunar Cycle: ....

Astrological Season:

....

Retrogrades:

....

Eclipses:

....

Other Events:

....

....

Takeaways from Today's Horoscope:

....
....
....
....
....
....
....
....
....
....
....
....
....

How I Felt

Start of the Day:

End of the Day:

Reflect

Did today's horoscope come true? ◯ Yes ◯ No
◯ Partially ....
....

What happened today?

....
....
....
....
....
....
....
....
....
....
....
....
....
....

What were my key takeaways from today's experiences?

....
....
....
....
....
....
....
....
....
....
....
....

What key astrological events influenced today?

....
....
....
....
....
....
....
....
....
....

Other Notes for Today:

Record

Date: Day of the Week: Time:

Today's Astrology:

Lunar Cycle: ....

Astrological Season:

....

Retrogrades:

....

Eclipses:

....

Other Events:

....

....

Takeaways from Today's Horoscope:

....
....
....
....
....
....
....
....
....
....
....

How I Felt

Start of the Day:

End of the Day:

Reflect

Did today's horoscope come true? ◯ Yes   ◯ No
◯ Partially ....
....

What happened today?

....
....
....
....
....
....
....
....
....
....
....
....
....
....

What were my key takeaways from today's experiences?

....
....
....
....
....
....
....
....
....
....
....
....

What key astrological events influenced today?

....
....
....
....
....
....
....
....
....
....

Other Notes for Today:

Record

Date: Day of the Week: Time:

Today's Astrology:

Lunar Cycle: ....

Astrological Season:
....

Retrogrades:
....

Eclipses:
....

Other Events:
....
....

Takeaways from Today's Horoscope:

....
....
....
....
....
....
....
....
....
....
....

How I Felt

Start of the Day:

End of the Day:

Reflect

Did today's horoscope come true?   ○ Yes   ○ No
○ Partially ....
....

What happened today?

....
....
....
....
....
....
....
....
....
....
....
....
....

What were my key takeaways from today's experiences?

....
....
....
....
....
....
....
....
....
....

What key astrological events influenced today?

....
....
....
....
....
....
....
....
....

Other Notes for Today:

Record

Date: Day of the Week: Time:

Today's Astrology:

Lunar Cycle: ....

Astrological Season:

....

Retrogrades:

....

Eclipses:

....

Other Events:

....

....

Takeaways from Today's Horoscope:

....

....

....

....

....

....

....

....

....

....

....

....

How I Felt

Start of the Day:

End of the Day:

Reflect

Did today's horoscope come true? ○ Yes ○ No
○ Partially ....
....

What happened today?

....
....
....
....
....
....
....
....
....
....
....
....
....
....

What were my key takeaways from today's experiences?

....
....
....
....
....
....
....
....
....
....
....

What key astrological events influenced today?

....
....
....
....
....
....
....
....
....
....

Other Notes for Today:

Record

Date:	Day of the Week:	Time:

Today's Astrology:

Lunar Cycle:...

Astrological Season:
....

Retrogrades:
....

Eclipses:
....

Other Events:
....
....

Takeaways from Today's Horoscope:

....
....
....
....
....
....
....
....
....
....
....
....
....
....

How I Felt

Start of the Day:

End of the Day:

Reflect

Did today's horoscope come true?   ○ Yes   ○ No
○ Partially ....

What happened today?

....
....
....
....
....
....
....
....
....
....
....
....
....
....
....

What were my key takeaways from today's experiences?

....
....
....
....
....
....
....
....
....
....
....

What key astrological events influenced today?

....
....
....
....
....
....
....
....
....

Other Notes for Today:

Record

Date: Day of the Week: Time:

Today's Astrology:

Lunar Cycle:...

Astrological Season:

....

Retrogrades:

....

Eclipses:

....

Other Events:

....

....

Takeaways from Today's Horoscope:

....
....
....
....
....
....
....
....
....
....
....
....

How I Felt

Start of the Day:

End of the Day:

Reflect

Did today's horoscope come true?   ○ Yes   ○ No
○ Partially

What happened today?

What were my key takeaways from today's experiences?

What key astrological events influenced today?

Other Notes for Today:

Record

Date: Day of the Week: Time:

Today's Astrology:

Lunar Cycle:..

Astrological Season:

....

Retrogrades:

....

Eclipses:

....

Other Events:

....

....

Takeaways from Today's Horoscope:

....
....
....
....
....
....
....
....
....
....
....
....
....

How I Felt

Start of the Day:

End of the Day:

Reflect

Did today's horoscope come true?   ○ Yes   ○ No
○ Partially ....
....

What happened today?

....
....
....
....
....
....
....
....
....
....
....
....
....

What were my key takeaways from today's experiences?

....
....
....
....
....
....
....
....
....
....
....

What key astrological events influenced today?

....
....
....
....
....
....
....
....
....

Other Notes for Today:

Record

Date: Day of the Week: Time:

Today's Astrology:

Lunar Cycle:..

Astrological Season:

....

Retrogrades:

....

Eclipses:

....

Other Events:

....

....

Takeaways from Today's Horoscope:

....
....
....
....
....
....
....
....
....
....

How I Felt

Start of the Day:

End of the Day:

Reflect

Did today's horoscope come true? ○ Yes ○ No
○ Partially ....
....

What happened today?

....
....
....
....
....
....
....
....
....
....
....
....
....
....
....
....

What were my key takeaways from today's experiences?

....
....
....
....
....
....
....
....
....
....
....
....

What key astrological events influenced today?

....
....
....
....
....
....
....
....
....
....

Other Notes for Today:

Record

Date: Day of the Week: Time:

Today's Astrology:

Lunar Cycle: ....

Astrological Season:

....

Retrogrades:

....

Eclipses:

....

Other Events:

....

....

Takeaways from Today's Horoscope:

....
....
....
....
....
....
....
....
....
....
....
....

How I Felt

Start of the Day:

End of the Day:

Reflect

Did today's horoscope come true? ○ Yes   ○ No
○ Partially ....
....

What happened today?
....
....
....
....
....
....
....
....
....
....
....
....
....
....
....

What were my key takeaways from today's experiences?
....
....
....
....
....
....
....
....
....
....
....

What key astrological events influenced today?
....
....
....
....
....
....
....
....
....
....

Other Notes for Today:

Record

Date: Day of the Week: Time:

Today's Astrology:

Lunar Cycle: ....

Astrological Season:

....

Retrogrades:

....

Eclipses:

....

Other Events:

....

....

Takeaways from Today's Horoscope:

....
....
....
....
....
....
....
....
....
....

How I Felt

Start of the Day:

End of the Day:

Reflect

Did today's horoscope come true? ⚪ Yes ⚪ No
⚪ Partially ....
....

What happened today?

....
....
....
....
....
....
....
....
....
....
....
....

What were my key takeaways from today's experiences?

....
....
....
....
....
....
....
....
....
....
....

What key astrological events influenced today?

....
....
....
....
....
....
....
....
....
....

Other Notes for Today:

Record

Date:	Day of the Week:	Time:

Today's Astrology:

Lunar Cycle:...

Astrological Season:

....

Retrogrades:

....

Eclipses:

....

Other Events:

....

....

Takeaways from Today's Horoscope:

....
....
....
....
....
....
....
....
....
....
....
....
....
....
....

How I Felt

Start of the Day:

End of the Day:

Reflect

Did today's horoscope come true? ◯ Yes ◯ No
◯ Partially ....
....

What happened today?

....
....
....
....
....
....
....
....
....
....
....
....
....
....

What were my key takeaways from today's experiences?

....
....
....
....
....
....
....
....
....
....
....
....

What key astrological events influenced today?

....
....
....
....
....
....
....
....
....

Other Notes for Today:

Record

Date: Day of the Week: Time:

Today's Astrology:

Lunar Cycle:...

Astrological Season:

....

Retrogrades:

....

Eclipses:

....

Other Events:

....

....

Takeaways from Today's Horoscope:

....
....
....
....
....
....
....
....
....
....
....
....

How I Felt

Start of the Day:

End of the Day:

Reflect

Did today's horoscope come true?   ◯ Yes   ◯ No
◯ Partially ....
....

What happened today?

....
....
....
....
....
....
....
....
....
....
....
....
....
....
....
....

What were my key takeaways from today's experiences?

....
....
....
....
....
....
....
....
....
....
....
....

What key astrological events influenced today?

....
....
....
....
....
....
....
....
....

Other Notes for Today:

Record

Date: Day of the Week: Time:

Today's Astrology:

Lunar Cycle: ....

Astrological Season:

....

Retrogrades:

....

Eclipses:

....

Other Events:

....
....

Takeaways from Today's Horoscope:

....
....
....
....
....
....
....
....
....
....
....
....

How I Felt

Start of the Day:

End of the Day:

Reflect

Did today's horoscope come true? ○ Yes ○ No
○ Partially ....
....

What happened today?

....
....
....
....
....
....
....
....
....
....
....
....

What were my key takeaways from today's experiences?

....
....
....
....
....
....
....
....
....

What key astrological events influenced today?

....
....
....
....
....
....

Other Notes for Today:

Record

Date: Day of the Week: Time:

Today's Astrology:

Lunar Cycle: ....

Astrological Season:

....

Retrogrades:

....

Eclipses:

....

Other Events:

....

....

Takeaways from Today's Horoscope:

....
....
....
....
....
....
....
....
....
....
....
....

How I Felt

Start of the Day:

End of the Day:

Reflect

Did today's horoscope come true? ○ Yes   ○ No
○ Partially ....

What happened today?

....
....
....
....
....
....
....
....
....
....
....
....
....

What were my key takeaways from today's experiences?

....
....
....
....
....
....
....
....
....

What key astrological events influenced today?

....
....
....
....
....
....
....
....

Other Notes for Today:

Record

Date: Day of the Week: Time:

Today's Astrology:

Lunar Cycle: ....

Astrological Season:
....

Retrogrades:
....

Eclipses:
....

Other Events:
....
....

Takeaways from Today's Horoscope:

....
....
....
....
....
....
....
....
....
....
....

How I Felt

Start of the Day:

End of the Day:

Reflect

Did today's horoscope come true? ◯ Yes ◯ No
◯ Partially ....
....

What happened today?

....
....
....
....
....
....
....
....
....
....
....
....
....
....
....

What were my key takeaways from today's experiences?

....
....
....
....
....
....
....
....
....
....
....
....

What key astrological events influenced today?

....
....
....
....
....
....
....
....
....
....
....

Other Notes for Today:

Record

Date:	Day of the Week:	Time:

Today's Astrology:

Lunar Cycle: ....

Astrological Season:
....

Retrogrades:
....

Eclipses:
....

Other Events:
....
....

Takeaways from Today's Horoscope:

....
....
....
....
....
....
....
....
....
....
....
....

How I Felt

Start of the Day:

End of the Day:

Reflect

Did today's horoscope come true?   ○ Yes   ○ No
○ Partially ....

What happened today?

....
....
....
....
....
....
....
....
....
....
....
....
....

What were my key takeaways from today's experiences?

....
....
....
....
....
....
....
....
....
....

What key astrological events influenced today?

....
....
....
....
....
....
....
....
....

Other Notes for Today:

Record

Date:	Day of the Week:	Time:

Today's Astrology:

Lunar Cycle:..

Astrological Season:

....

Retrogrades:

....

Eclipses:

....

Other Events:

....

....

Takeaways from Today's Horoscope:

....
....
....
....
....
....
....
....
....
....
....
....

How I Felt

Start of the Day:

End of the Day:

Reflect

Did today's horoscope come true? ○ Yes ○ No
○ Partially ....
....

What happened today?
....
....
....
....
....
....
....
....
....
....
....
....
....

What were my key takeaways from today's experiences?
....
....
....
....
....
....
....
....
....
....

What key astrological events influenced today?
....
....
....
....
....
....
....
....
....
....

Other Notes for Today:

Record

Date: Day of the Week: Time:

Today's Astrology:

Lunar Cycle: ....

Astrological Season:
....

Retrogrades:
....

Eclipses:
....

Other Events:
....
....

Takeaways from Today's Horoscope:

....
....
....
....
....
....
....
....
....
....
....
....

How I Felt

Start of the Day:

End of the Day:

Reflect

Did today's horoscope come true? ◯ Yes ◯ No
◯ Partially

What happened today?

What were my key takeaways from today's experiences?

What key astrological events influenced today?

Other Notes for Today:

·85·

Record

Date: Day of the Week: Time:

Today's Astrology:

Lunar Cycle:

Astrological Season:

Retrogrades:

Eclipses:

Other Events:

Takeaways from Today's Horoscope:

How I Felt

Start of the Day:

End of the Day:

Reflect

Did today's horoscope come true? ○ Yes   ○ No
○ Partially ....

What happened today?

....
....
....
....
....
....
....
....
....
....
....
....
....
....
....
....

What were my key takeaways from today's experiences?

....
....
....
....
....
....
....
....
....
....
....
....
....

What key astrological events influenced today?

....
....
....
....
....
....
....
....
....
....

Other Notes for Today:

Record

Date: Day of the Week: Time:

Today's Astrology:

Lunar Cycle: ....

Astrological Season:
....

Retrogrades:
....

Eclipses:
....

Other Events:
....
....

Takeaways from Today's Horoscope:

....
....
....
....
....
....
....
....
....
....
....
....

How I Felt

Start of the Day:

End of the Day:

Reflect

Did today's horoscope come true? ○ Yes ○ No
○ Partially ....
....

What happened today?
....
....
....
....
....
....
....
....
....
....
....
....

What were my key takeaways from today's experiences?
....
....
....
....
....
....
....
....
....

What key astrological events influenced today?
....
....
....
....
....
....
....
....
....

Other Notes for Today:

Record

Date:	Day of the Week:	Time:

Today's Astrology:

Lunar Cycle:...

Astrological Season:
....

Retrogrades:
....

Eclipses:
....

Other Events:
....
....

Takeaways from Today's Horoscope:

....
....
....
....
....
....
....
....
....
....
....

How I Felt

Start of the Day:

End of the Day:

Reflect

Did today's horoscope come true?   ◯ Yes   ◯ No
◯ Partially ....
....

What happened today?

....
....
....
....
....
....
....
....
....
....
....
....
....
....
....
....

What were my key takeaways from today's experiences?

....
....
....
....
....
....
....
....
....
....
....

What key astrological events influenced today?

....
....
....
....
....
....
....
....
....

Other Notes for Today:

Record

Date: Day of the Week: Time:

Today's Astrology:

Lunar Cycle:...................................

Astrological Season:

....

Retrogrades:

....

Eclipses:

....

Other Events:

....

....

Takeaways from Today's Horoscope:

....
....
....
....
....
....
....
....
....
....
....
....

How I Felt

Start of the Day:

End of the Day:

Reflect

Did today's horoscope come true? ○ Yes ○ No
○ Partially ....
....

What happened today?

....
....
....
....
....
....
....
....
....
....
....
....
....
....

What were my key takeaways from today's experiences?

....
....
....
....
....
....
....
....
....
....
....

What key astrological events influenced today?

....
....
....
....
....
....
....
....
....
....

Other Notes for Today:

Record

Date: Day of the Week: Time:

Today's Astrology:

Lunar Cycle:...

Astrological Season:

....

Retrogrades:

....

Eclipses:

....

Other Events:

....

....

Takeaways from Today's Horoscope:

....
....
....
....
....
....
....
....
....
....
....
....

How I Felt

Start of the Day:

End of the Day:

Reflect

Did today's horoscope come true? ○ Yes ○ No
○ Partially ....
....

What happened today?

....
....
....
....
....
....
....
....
....
....
....
....
....
....

What were my key takeaways from today's experiences?

....
....
....
....
....
....
....
....
....
....
....
....

What key astrological events influenced today?

....
....
....
....
....
....
....
....
....
....

Other Notes for Today:

Record

Date: Day of the Week: Time:

Today's Astrology:

Lunar Cycle: ....

Astrological Season:

....

Retrogrades:

....

Eclipses:

....

Other Events:

....

....

Takeaways from Today's Horoscope:

....
....
....
....
....
....
....
....
....
....

How I Felt

Start of the Day:

End of the Day:

Reflect

Did today's horoscope come true?   ○ Yes   ○ No
○ Partially

What happened today?

What were my key takeaways from today's experiences?

What key astrological events influenced today?

Other Notes for Today:

Record

Date: Day of the Week: Time:

Today's Astrology:

Lunar Cycle:...

Astrological Season:

....

Retrogrades:

....

Eclipses:

....

Other Events:

....

....

Takeaways from Today's Horoscope:

....
....
....
....
....
....
....
....
....
....
....
....
....
....

How I Felt

Start of the Day:

End of the Day:

Reflect

Did today's horoscope come true? ○ Yes ○ No
○ Partially ....
....

What happened today?

....
....
....
....
....
....
....
....
....
....
....
....
....
....
....

What were my key takeaways from today's experiences?

....
....
....
....
....
....
....
....
....
....
....
....

What key astrological events influenced today?

....
....
....
....
....
....
....
....
....

Other Notes for Today:

Record

Date: Day of the Week: Time:

Today's Astrology:

Lunar Cycle: ....

Astrological Season:

....

Retrogrades:

....

Eclipses:

....

Other Events:

....

....

Takeaways from Today's Horoscope:

....
....
....
....
....
....
....
....
....
....
....
....

How I Felt

Start of the Day:

End of the Day:

Reflect

Did today's horoscope come true? ○ Yes ○ No
○ Partially ....
....

What happened today?

....
....
....
....
....
....
....
....
....
....
....
....

What were my key takeaways from today's experiences?

....
....
....
....
....
....
....
....
....
....
....

What key astrological events influenced today?

....
....
....
....
....
....
....
....

Other Notes for Today:

Record

| Date: | Day of the Week: | Time: |

Today's Astrology:

Lunar Cycle:..

Astrological Season:
....

Retrogrades:
....

Eclipses:
....

Other Events:
....
....

Takeaways from Today's Horoscope:

....
....
....
....
....
....
....
....
....
....
....
....

How I Felt

Start of the Day:

End of the Day:

Reflect

Did today's horoscope come true? ◯ Yes   ◯ No
◯ Partially ....
....

What happened today?

....
....
....
....
....
....
....
....
....
....
....
....
....
....
....

What were my key takeaways from today's experiences?

....
....
....
....
....
....
....
....
....
....
....
....
....

What key astrological events influenced today?

....
....
....
....
....
....
....
....
....
....
....
....

Other Notes for Today:

Record

Date: Day of the Week: Time:

Today's Astrology:

Lunar Cycle: ....

Astrological Season:

....

Retrogrades:

....

Eclipses:

....

Other Events:

....

....

Takeaways from Today's Horoscope:

....
....
....
....
....
....
....
....
....
....
....
....

How I Felt

Start of the Day:

End of the Day:

Reflect

Did today's horoscope come true?   ○ Yes   ○ No
○ Partially ....
....

What happened today?

....
....
....
....
....
....
....
....
....
....
....
....
....
....
....

What were my key takeaways from today's experiences?

....
....
....
....
....
....
....
....
....
....
....

What key astrological events influenced today?

....
....
....
....
....
....
....
....
....

Other Notes for Today:

Record

Date: Day of the Week: Time:

Today's Astrology:

Lunar Cycle:..

Astrological Season:
....

Retrogrades:
....

Eclipses:
....

Other Events:
....
....

Takeaways from Today's Horoscope:

....
....
....
....
....
....
....
....
....
....
....
....

How I Felt

Start of the Day:

End of the Day:

Reflect

Did today's horoscope come true?   ○ Yes   ○ No
○ Partially ....
....

What happened today?

....
....
....
....
....
....
....
....
....
....
....
....
....
....

What were my key takeaways from today's experiences?

....
....
....
....
....
....
....
....
....
....

What key astrological events influenced today?

....
....
....
....
....
....
....
....

Other Notes for Today:

Record

Date:	Day of the Week:	Time:

Today's Astrology:

Lunar Cycle: ....

Astrological Season:

....

Retrogrades:

....

Eclipses:

....

Other Events:

....

....

Takeaways from Today's Horoscope:

....
....
....
....
....
....
....
....
....
....
....
....

How I Felt

Start of the Day:

End of the Day:

Reflect

Did today's horoscope come true?   ○ Yes   ○ No
○ Partially ....

What happened today?

What were my key takeaways from today's experiences?

What key astrological events influenced today?

Other Notes for Today:

Record

Date: Day of the Week: Time:

Today's Astrology:

Lunar Cycle:...

Astrological Season:

....

Retrogrades:

....

Eclipses:

....

Other Events:

....

....

Takeaways from Today's Horoscope:

....
....
....
....
....
....
....
....
....
....
....
....
....
....

How I Felt

Start of the Day:

End of the Day:

Reflect

Did today's horoscope come true? ○ Yes ○ No
○ Partially ....

What happened today?

....
....
....
....
....
....
....
....
....
....
....
....
....
....
....
....
....
....

What were my key takeaways from today's experiences?

....
....
....
....
....
....
....
....
....
....
....
....
....

What key astrological events influenced today?

....
....
....
....
....
....
....
....
....
....
....

Other Notes for Today:

Record

Date:	Day of the Week:	Time:

Today's Astrology:

Lunar Cycle:...

Astrological Season:

Retrogrades:

Eclipses:

Other Events:

Takeaways from Today's Horoscope:

How I Felt

Start of the Day:

End of the Day:

Reflect

Did today's horoscope come true? ○ Yes ○ No
○ Partially ....
....

What happened today?

....
....
....
....
....
....
....
....
....
....
....
....
....
....

What were my key takeaways from today's experiences?

....
....
....
....
....
....
....
....
....
....
....
....

What key astrological events influenced today?

....
....
....
....
....
....
....
....
....
....
....

Other Notes for Today:

Record

Date: Day of the Week: Time:

Today's Astrology:

Lunar Cycle:..

Astrological Season:

....

Retrogrades:

....

Eclipses:

....

Other Events:

....

....

Takeaways from Today's Horoscope:

....
....
....
....
....
....
....
....
....
....
....

How I Felt

Start of the Day:

End of the Day:

Reflect

Did today's horoscope come true? ◯ Yes ◯ No
◯ Partially ....

What happened today?

....
....
....
....
....
....
....
....
....
....
....
....
....

What were my key takeaways from today's experiences?

....
....
....
....
....
....
....
....
....
....
....

What key astrological events influenced today?

....
....
....
....
....
....
....
....
....
....

Other Notes for Today:

Record

Date: Day of the Week: Time:

Today's Astrology:

Lunar Cycle: ....

Astrological Season:

....

Retrogrades:

....

Eclipses:

....

Other Events:

....

....

Takeaways from Today's Horoscope:

....
....
....
....
....
....
....
....
....
....
....
....

How I Felt

Start of the Day:

End of the Day:

Reflect

Did today's horoscope come true? ○ Yes   ○ No
○ Partially

What happened today?

What were my key takeaways from today's experiences?

What key astrological events influenced today?

Other Notes for Today:

Record

Date: Day of the Week: Time:

Today's Astrology:

Lunar Cycle:...

Astrological Season:

....

Retrogrades:

....

Eclipses:

....

Other Events:

....

....

Takeaways from Today's Horoscope:

....
....
....
....
....
....
....
....
....
....
....
....

How I Felt

Start of the Day:

End of the Day:

Reflect

Did today's horoscope come true?   ○ Yes   ○ No
○ Partially ....
....

What happened today?

....
....
....
....
....
....
....
....
....
....
....
....
....

What were my key takeaways from today's experiences?

....
....
....
....
....
....
....
....
....
....
....

What key astrological events influenced today?

....
....
....
....
....
....
....
....

Other Notes for Today:

Record

Date: Day of the Week: Time:

Today's Astrology:

Lunar Cycle: ....

Astrological Season:

....

Retrogrades:

....

Eclipses:

....

Other Events:

....

....

Takeaways from Today's Horoscope:

....
....
....
....
....
....
....
....
....
....
....

How I Felt

Start of the Day:

End of the Day:

Reflect

Did today's horoscope come true? ○ Yes ○ No
○ Partially ....
....

What happened today?

....
....
....
....
....
....
....
....
....
....
....
....
....
....

What were my key takeaways from today's experiences?

....
....
....
....
....
....
....
....
....
....

What key astrological events influenced today?

....
....
....
....
....
....
....
....
....

Other Notes for Today:

Record

Date: Day of the Week: Time:

Today's Astrology:

Lunar Cycle:..

Astrological Season:
....

Retrogrades:
....

Eclipses:
....

Other Events:
....
....

Takeaways from Today's Horoscope:

....
....
....
....
....
....
....
....
....
....
....

How I Felt

Start of the Day:

End of the Day:

Reflect

Did today's horoscope come true? ◯ Yes ◯ No
◯ Partially

What happened today?

What were my key takeaways from today's experiences?

What key astrological events influenced today?

Other Notes for Today:

Record

Date: Day of the Week: Time:

Today's Astrology:

Lunar Cycle: ....

Astrological Season:

....

Retrogrades:

....

Eclipses:

....

Other Events:

....

....

Takeaways from Today's Horoscope:

....
....
....
....
....
....
....
....
....
....
....
....

How I Felt

Start of the Day:

End of the Day:

Reflect

Did today's horoscope come true? ○ Yes ○ No
○ Partially ....
....

What happened today?

....
....
....
....
....
....
....
....
....
....
....
....
....
....

What were my key takeaways from today's experiences?

....
....
....
....
....
....
....
....
....
....

What key astrological events influenced today?

....
....
....
....
....
....
....
....
....

Other Notes for Today:

Record

Date: Day of the Week: Time:

Today's Astrology:

Lunar Cycle: ....

Astrological Season:
....

Retrogrades:
....

Eclipses:
....

Other Events:
....
....

Takeaways from Today's Horoscope:

....
....
....
....
....
....
....
....
....
....
....

How I Felt

Start of the Day:

End of the Day:

Reflect

Did today's horoscope come true? ○ Yes ○ No
○ Partially ....

What happened today?

....
....
....
....
....
....
....
....
....
....
....
....
....
....
....

What were my key takeaways from today's experiences?

....
....
....
....
....
....
....
....
....
....
....

What key astrological events influenced today?

....
....
....
....
....
....
....
....
....
....

Other Notes for Today:

Record

Date: Day of the Week: Time:

Today's Astrology:

Lunar Cycle: ....

Astrological Season:

....

Retrogrades:

....

Eclipses:

....

Other Events:

....

....

Takeaways from Today's Horoscope:

....
....
....
....
....
....
....
....
....
....
....
....

How I Felt

Start of the Day:

End of the Day:

Reflect

Did today's horoscope come true? ◯ Yes ◯ No
◯ Partially ....
....

What happened today?

....
....
....
....
....
....
....
....
....
....
....
....
....
....

What were my key takeaways from today's experiences?

....
....
....
....
....
....
....
....
....
....
....

What key astrological events influenced today?

....
....
....
....
....
....
....
....
....

Other Notes for Today:

Record

Date: _____ Day of the Week: _____ Time: _____

Today's Astrology:

Lunar Cycle: ....

Astrological Season:

....

Retrogrades:

....

Eclipses:

....

Other Events:

....

....

Takeaways from Today's Horoscope:

....
....
....
....
....
....
....
....
....
....
....
....
....
....
....
....
....

How I Felt

Start of the Day:

End of the Day:

Reflect

Did today's horoscope come true?   ○ Yes   ○ No
○ Partially ....
....

What happened today?

....
....
....
....
....
....
....
....
....
....
....
....
....
....
....

What were my key takeaways from today's experiences?

....
....
....
....
....
....
....
....
....
....
....
....

What key astrological events influenced today?

....
....
....
....
....
....
....
....
....
....

Other Notes for Today:

Record

Date: Day of the Week: Time:

Today's Astrology:

Lunar Cycle: ....

Astrological Season:
....

Retrogrades:
....

Eclipses:
....

Other Events:
....
....

Takeaways from Today's Horoscope:

....
....
....
....
....
....
....
....
....
....

How I Felt

Start of the Day:

End of the Day:

Reflect

Did today's horoscope come true? ◯ Yes ◯ No
◯ Partially ....

What happened today?

....
....
....
....
....
....
....
....
....
....
....
....
....

What were my key takeaways from today's experiences?

....
....
....
....
....
....
....
....
....
....

What key astrological events influenced today?

....
....
....
....
....
....
....
....
....
....

Other Notes for Today:

Record

Date: Day of the Week: Time:

Today's Astrology:

Lunar Cycle: ....

Astrological Season:

....

Retrogrades:

....

Eclipses:

....

Other Events:

....

....

Takeaways from Today's Horoscope:

....
....
....
....
....
....
....
....
....
....
....
....

How I Felt

Start of the Day:

End of the Day:

Reflect

Did today's horoscope come true? ○ Yes ○ No
○ Partially ....
....

What happened today?

....
....
....
....
....
....
....
....
....
....
....
....
....
....

What were my key takeaways from today's experiences?

....
....
....
....
....
....
....
....
....
....
....

What key astrological events influenced today?

....
....
....
....
....
....
....
....
....

Other Notes for Today:

Record

Date: Day of the Week: Time:

Today's Astrology:

Lunar Cycle:...

Astrological Season:

....

Retrogrades:

....

Eclipses:

....

Other Events:

....

....

Takeaways from Today's Horoscope:

....
....
....
....
....
....
....
....
....
....

How I Felt

Start of the Day:

End of the Day:

Reflect

Did today's horoscope come true?   ◯ Yes   ◯ No
◯ Partially ....
....

What happened today?

....
....
....
....
....
....
....
....
....
....
....
....
....

What were my key takeaways from today's experiences?

....
....
....
....
....
....
....
....
....
....

What key astrological events influenced today?

....
....
....
....
....
....
....
....
....

Other Notes for Today:

Record

Date: Day of the Week: Time:

Today's Astrology:

Lunar Cycle:...

Astrological Season:

....

Retrogrades:

....

Eclipses:

....

Other Events:

....

....

Takeaways from Today's Horoscope:

....
....
....
....
....
....
....
....
....
....
....
....
....

How I Felt

Start of the Day:

End of the Day:

Reflect

Did today's horoscope come true? ◯ Yes ◯ No
◯ Partially

What happened today?

What were my key takeaways from today's experiences?

What key astrological events influenced today?

Other Notes for Today:

Record

Date: Day of the Week: Time:

Today's Astrology:

Lunar Cycle:....................................

Astrological Season:
....

Retrogrades:
....

Eclipses:
....

Other Events:
....
....

Takeaways from Today's Horoscope:

....
....
....
....
....
....
....
....
....
....

How I Felt

Start of the Day:

End of the Day:

Reflect

Did today's horoscope come true?   ○ Yes   ○ No
○ Partially ....

What happened today?

What were my key takeaways from today's experiences?

What key astrological events influenced today?

Other Notes for Today:

Record

Date:	Day of the Week:	Time:

Today's Astrology:

Lunar Cycle: ....

Astrological Season:

....

Retrogrades:

....

Eclipses:

....

Other Events:

....

....

Takeaways from Today's Horoscope:

....
....
....
....
....
....
....
....
....
....
....
....

How I Felt

Start of the Day:

End of the Day:

Reflect

Did today's horoscope come true? ○ Yes ○ No
○ Partially ....
....

What happened today?

....
....
....
....
....
....
....
....
....
....
....
....
....
....

What were my key takeaways from today's experiences?

....
....
....
....
....
....
....
....
....
....
....
....

What key astrological events influenced today?

....
....
....
....
....
....
....
....
....

Other Notes for Today:

Record

Date:	Day of the Week:	Time:

Today's Astrology:

Lunar Cycle: ....

Astrological Season:
....

Retrogrades:
....

Eclipses:
....

Other Events:
....
....

Takeaways from Today's Horoscope:

....
....
....
....
....
....
....
....
....

How I Felt

Start of the Day:

End of the Day:

Reflect

Did today's horoscope come true? ◯ Yes ◯ No
◯ Partially ....
....

What happened today?

....
....
....
....
....
....
....
....
....
....
....
....
....

What were my key takeaways from today's experiences?

....
....
....
....
....
....
....
....
....
....

What key astrological events influenced today?

....
....
....
....
....
....
....
....
....
....

Other Notes for Today:

Record

Date: Day of the Week: Time:

Today's Astrology:

Lunar Cycle: ....

Astrological Season:

....

Retrogrades:

....

Eclipses:

....

Other Events:

....

....

Takeaways from Today's Horoscope:

....
....
....
....
....
....
....
....
....
....
....

How I Felt

Start of the Day:

End of the Day:

Reflect

Did today's horoscope come true? ◯ Yes ◯ No
◯ Partially ....

What happened today?

....
....
....
....
....
....
....
....
....
....
....
....
....

What were my key takeaways from today's experiences?

....
....
....
....
....
....
....
....
....

What key astrological events influenced today?

....
....
....
....
....
....
....
....
....

Other Notes for Today:

Record

Date: Day of the Week: Time:

Today's Astrology:

Lunar Cycle:....................................

Astrological Season:

....

Retrogrades:

....

Eclipses:

....

Other Events:

....

....

Takeaways from Today's Horoscope:

....
....
....
....
....
....
....
....
....
....
....
....

How I Felt

Start of the Day:

End of the Day:

Reflect

Did today's horoscope come true? ◯ Yes   ◯ No
◯ Partially ....

What happened today?

....
....
....
....
....
....
....
....
....
....
....
....
....

What were my key takeaways from today's experiences?

....
....
....
....
....
....
....
....
....
....

What key astrological events influenced today?

....
....
....
....
....
....
....
....

Other Notes for Today:

Record

Date: Day of the Week: Time:

Today's Astrology:

Lunar Cycle:

Astrological Season:

Retrogrades:

Eclipses:

Other Events:

Takeaways from Today's Horoscope:

How I Felt

Start of the Day:

End of the Day:

Reflect

Did today's horoscope come true? ◯ Yes ◯ No
◯ Partially ....

What happened today?

....
....
....
....
....
....
....
....
....
....
....
....
....
....

What were my key takeaways from today's experiences?

....
....
....
....
....
....
....
....
....
....
....

What key astrological events influenced today?

....
....
....
....
....
....
....
....
....
....

Other Notes for Today:

Record

Date: Day of the Week: Time:

Today's Astrology:

Lunar Cycle: ....

Astrological Season:
....

Retrogrades:
....

Eclipses:
....

Other Events:
....
....

Takeaways from Today's Horoscope:

....
....
....
....
....
....
....
....
....
....
....
....
....
....

How I Felt

Start of the Day:

End of the Day:

Reflect

Did today's horoscope come true?   ○ Yes   ○ No
○ Partially ....

....

What happened today?

....
....
....
....
....
....
....
....
....
....
....
....
....
....
....

What were my key takeaways from today's experiences?

....
....
....
....
....
....
....
....
....
....
....
....

What key astrological events influenced today?

....
....
....
....
....
....
....
....
....
....

Other Notes for Today:

Record

Date:	Day of the Week:	Time:

Today's Astrology:

Lunar Cycle:..

Astrological Season:
....

Retrogrades:
....

Eclipses:
....

Other Events:
....
....

Takeaways from Today's Horoscope:

....
....
....
....
....
....
....
....
....
....
....
....

How I Felt

Start of the Day:

End of the Day:

Reflect

Did today's horoscope come true? ○ Yes ○ No
○ Partially ....
....

What happened today?
....
....
....
....
....
....
....
....
....
....
....
....
....
....

What were my key takeaways from today's experiences?
....
....
....
....
....
....
....
....
....
....
....

What key astrological events influenced today?
....
....
....
....
....
....
....
....
....
....
....
....

Other Notes for Today:

Record

Date: Day of the Week: Time:

Today's Astrology:

Lunar Cycle:...

Astrological Season:

....

Retrogrades:

....

Eclipses:

....

Other Events:

....

....

Takeaways from Today's Horoscope:

....
....
....
....
....
....
....
....
....
....
....

How I Felt

Start of the Day:

End of the Day:

Reflect

Did today's horoscope come true? ○ Yes ○ No
○ Partially ....

What happened today?

....
....
....
....
....
....
....
....
....
....
....
....
....
....
....

What were my key takeaways from today's experiences?

....
....
....
....
....
....
....
....
....
....
....
....

What key astrological events influenced today?

....
....
....
....
....
....
....
....
....

Other Notes for Today:

Record

Date: Day of the Week: Time:

Today's Astrology:

Lunar Cycle: ....

Astrological Season:
....

Retrogrades:
....

Eclipses:
....

Other Events:
....
....

Takeaways from Today's Horoscope:

....
....
....
....
....
....
....
....
....
....
....
....

How I Felt

Start of the Day:

End of the Day:

Reflect

Did today's horoscope come true? ○ Yes ○ No
○ Partially ....

What happened today?

....
....
....
....
....
....
....
....
....
....
....
....
....
....
....
....

What were my key takeaways from today's experiences?

....
....
....
....
....
....
....
....
....
....
....
....

What key astrological events influenced today?

....
....
....
....
....
....
....
....
....
....

Other Notes for Today:

Record

Date: Day of the Week: Time:

Today's Astrology:

Lunar Cycle:..

Astrological Season:

....

Retrogrades:

....

Eclipses:

....

Other Events:

....

....

Takeaways from Today's Horoscope:

....
....
....
....
....
....
....
....
....
....
....
....
....

How I Felt

Start of the Day:

End of the Day:

Reflect

Did today's horoscope come true? ○ Yes ○ No
○ Partially ....
....

What happened today?

....
....
....
....
....
....
....
....
....
....
....
....
....
....
....
....
....

What key astrological events influenced today?

....
....
....
....
....
....
....
....
....
....

What were my key takeaways from today's experiences?

....
....
....
....
....
....
....
....
....
....
....
....

Other Notes for Today:

Record

Date: Day of the Week: Time:

Today's Astrology:

Lunar Cycle:

Astrological Season:

Retrogrades:

Eclipses:

Other Events:

Takeaways from Today's Horoscope:

How I Felt

Start of the Day:

End of the Day:

Reflect

Did today's horoscope come true? ◯ Yes ◯ No
◯ Partially ....
....

What happened today?

....
....
....
....
....
....
....
....
....
....
....
....
....
....

What were my key takeaways from today's experiences?

....
....
....
....
....
....
....
....
....
....

What key astrological events influenced today?

....
....
....
....
....
....
....
....

Other Notes for Today:

Record

Date: | Day of the Week: | Time:

Today's Astrology:

Lunar Cycle: ....

Astrological Season:
....

Retrogrades:
....

Eclipses:
....

Other Events:
....
....

Takeaways from Today's Horoscope:

....
....
....
....
....
....
....
....
....
....
....
....
....
....

How I Felt

Start of the Day:

End of the Day:

Reflect

Did today's horoscope come true? ◯ Yes ◯ No
◯ Partially ....
....

What happened today?

....
....
....
....
....
....
....
....
....
....
....
....
....
....
....
....
....

What were my key takeaways from today's experiences?

....
....
....
....
....
....
....
....
....
....
....
....
....

What key astrological events influenced today?

....
....
....
....
....
....
....
....
....
....

Other Notes for Today:

Record

Date: Day of the Week: Time:

Today's Astrology:

Lunar Cycle:..

Astrological Season:

....

Retrogrades:

....

Eclipses:

....

Other Events:

....

....

Takeaways from Today's Horoscope:

....
....
....
....
....
....
....
....
....
....
....
....

How I Felt

Start of the Day:

End of the Day:

Reflect

Did today's horoscope come true? ◯ Yes ◯ No
◯ Partially ....
....

What happened today?

....
....
....
....
....
....
....
....
....
....
....
....
....
....
....

What were my key takeaways from today's experiences?

....
....
....
....
....
....
....
....
....
....

What key astrological events influenced today?

....
....
....
....
....
....
....
....
....
....

Other Notes for Today:

Record

Date: Day of the Week: Time:

Today's Astrology:

Lunar Cycle: ....

Astrological Season:
....

Retrogrades:
....

Eclipses:
....

Other Events:
....
....

Takeaways from Today's Horoscope:

....
....
....
....
....
....
....
....
....
....
....

How I Felt

Start of the Day:

End of the Day:

Reflect

Did today's horoscope come true?   ◯ Yes   ◯ No
◯ Partially ....
....

What happened today?

....
....
....
....
....
....
....
....
....
....
....
....
....
....

What were my key takeaways from today's experiences?

....
....
....
....
....
....
....
....
....
....
....
....

What key astrological events influenced today?

....
....
....
....
....
....
....
....

Other Notes for Today:

Record

Date: Day of the Week: Time:

Today's Astrology:

Lunar Cycle:......................................

Astrological Season:

....

Retrogrades:

....

Eclipses:

....

Other Events:

....

....

Takeaways from Today's Horoscope:

....
....
....
....
....
....
....
....
....
....
....
....

How I Felt

Start of the Day:

End of the Day:

Reflect

Did today's horoscope come true?　○ Yes　○ No
○ Partially ....
....

What happened today?

....
....
....
....
....
....
....
....
....
....
....
....
....

What were my key takeaways from today's experiences?

....
....
....
....
....
....
....
....
....
....
....

What key astrological events influenced today?

....
....
....
....
....
....
....
....
....
....

Other Notes for Today:

Record

Date: Day of the Week: Time:

Today's Astrology:

Lunar Cycle: ....

Astrological Season:
....

Retrogrades:
....

Eclipses:
....

Other Events:
....
....

Takeaways from Today's Horoscope:

....
....
....
....
....
....
....
....
....
....
....

How I Felt

Start of the Day:

End of the Day:

Reflect

Did today's horoscope come true?   ○ Yes   ○ No
○ Partially ....
....

What happened today?

....
....
....
....
....
....
....
....
....
....
....
....

What were my key takeaways from today's experiences?

....
....
....
....
....
....
....
....
....
....

What key astrological events influenced today?

....
....
....
....
....
....
....
....
....
....

Other Notes for Today:

Record

Date:	Day of the Week:	Time:

Today's Astrology:

Lunar Cycle: ....

Astrological Season:

....

Retrogrades:

....

Eclipses:

....

Other Events:

....

....

Takeaways from Today's Horoscope:

....

....

....

....

....

....

....

....

....

....

....

How I Felt

Start of the Day:

End of the Day:

Reflect

Did today's horoscope come true?   ◯ Yes   ◯ No
◯ Partially ....
....

What happened today?

....
....
....
....
....
....
....
....
....
....

What were my key takeaways from today's experiences?

....
....
....
....
....
....
....
....

What key astrological events influenced today?

....
....
....
....
....
....

Other Notes for Today:

Record

Date: Day of the Week: Time:

Today's Astrology:

Lunar Cycle: ....

Astrological Season:

....

Retrogrades:

....

Eclipses:

....

Other Events:

....

....

Takeaways from Today's Horoscope:

....
....
....
....
....
....
....
....
....
....
....
....

How I Felt

Start of the Day:

End of the Day:

Reflect

Did today's horoscope come true?   ◯ Yes   ◯ No
◯ Partially ....
....

What happened today?

....
....
....
....
....
....
....
....
....
....
....
....
....

What were my key takeaways from today's experiences?

....
....
....
....
....
....
....
....
....
....
....

What key astrological events influenced today?

....
....
....
....
....
....
....
....
....
....

Other Notes for Today:

Record

Date:	Day of the Week:	Time:

Today's Astrology:

Lunar Cycle: ....

Astrological Season:

....

Retrogrades:

....

Eclipses:

....

Other Events:

....

....

Takeaways from Today's Horoscope:

....
....
....
....
....
....
....
....
....
....
....
....

How I Felt

Start of the Day:

End of the Day:

Reflect

Did today's horoscope come true? ○ Yes ○ No
○ Partially

What happened today?

What were my key takeaways from today's experiences?

What key astrological events influenced today?

Other Notes for Today:

Record

Date: Day of the Week: Time:

Today's Astrology:

Lunar Cycle: ....

Astrological Season:

....

Retrogrades:

....

Eclipses:

....

Other Events:

....
....

Takeaways from Today's Horoscope:

....
....
....
....
....
....
....
....
....
....

How I Felt

Start of the Day:

End of the Day:

Reflect

Did today's horoscope come true?   ◯ Yes   ◯ No
◯ Partially ....
....

What happened today?

....
....
....
....
....
....
....
....
....
....
....
....
....

What were my key takeaways from today's experiences?

....
....
....
....
....
....
....
....
....
....

What key astrological events influenced today?

....
....
....
....
....
....
....
....

Other Notes for Today:

Record

Date: Day of the Week: Time:

Today's Astrology:

Lunar Cycle: ....

Astrological Season:

....

Retrogrades:

....

Eclipses:

....

Other Events:

....
....

Takeaways from Today's Horoscope:

....
....
....
....
....
....
....
....
....
....
....
....
....

How I Felt

Start of the Day:

End of the Day:

Reflect

Did today's horoscope come true? ◯ Yes ◯ No
◯ Partially

What happened today?

What were my key takeaways from today's experiences?

What key astrological events influenced today?

Other Notes for Today:

Record

Date: Day of the Week: Time:

Today's Astrology:

Lunar Cycle: ....

Astrological Season:
....

Retrogrades:
....

Eclipses:
....

Other Events:
....
....

Takeaways from Today's Horoscope:

....
....
....
....
....
....
....
....
....
....
....
....

How I Felt

Start of the Day:

End of the Day:

Reflect

Did today's horoscope come true? ◯ Yes ◯ No
◯ Partially ....
....

What happened today?
....
....
....
....
....
....
....
....
....
....
....
....
....
....
....

What were my key takeaways from today's experiences?
....
....
....
....
....
....
....
....
....
....
....

What key astrological events influenced today?
....
....
....
....
....
....
....
....
....

Other Notes for Today:

Resources

Books

A Little Bit of Astrology by Colin Bedell

Astrology for Yourself by Demetra George and Douglas Bloch

Astrology for the Light Side of the Brain by Kim Rogers-Gallagher

Astrology for the Light Side of the Future by Kim Rogers-Gallagher

Astrology for Real Life by Theresa Reed

Star Power by Vanessa Montgomery

Astrology for Happiness and Success by Mecca Woods

Podcasts

Stars On Fire

AstroFabulous with Nadiya Shah

The Strology Show

Ghost of a Podcast

Websites for Birth Charts, Astrology Articles, or Learning Astrology

www.astro.com

www.astro-seek.com

www.tarot.com

www.astrology.com

https://sagmind.wordpress.com

Apps

TimePassages

My Moon Phase

Classes and *YouTube* Channels

www.rebeccagordonastrology.com (classes)

https://unlockastrology.com (classes)

Stormie Grace Astrology (YouTube)

The Oraculos Podcast (YouTube)

Index

A

Air element, 11–12
Apps, 29, 40, 187
Aquarius, 11, 12, 21
Aries, 11, 12, 13
Astro.com, 40
Astro-Charts.com, 40
Astro-Seek.com, 29
Astrology
  basics of, 10–35
  birth chart and, 6–7, 11, 40
  for decision-making, 7, 9, 25
  elements and, 11–12
  explanation of, 6–7, 9
  horoscope and, 7, 40–41
  journal pages for, 42–185
  lunar cycle and, 23–25, 29, 40
  personal growth and, 28, 37–38, 41, 43
  planets and, 11, 28–35
  for predictions, 6
  qualities and, 11–13
  for self-care, 28, 33, 34, 39, 43
  solar cycle and, 26
  spiritual growth and, 37–38, 41, 43
  sun signs, 11–35
  understanding of, 37, 40–41
  uses for, 6-7, 9
Awareness, 35–38, 40

B

Birth chart
  app for, 40
  for journaling, 40
  as map, 6–7
  sun signs and, 6–7, 11, 40
  website for, 40
Bustle.com, 40

C

Cancer, 11, 12, 15–16
Capricorn, 11, 12, 20
Cardinal quality, 11, 12
Creativity, 12, 38
Cycles
  lunar cycle, 23–25, 29, 40
  patterns and, 6–7, 26
  planetary cycles, 6–7, 29–35, 37
  seasonal cycles, 6, 26, 37
  solar cycle, 26
  study of, 6
  tracking, 6–7, 37, 40

D

Daily Planetary Guide, 28
Decision-making, 7, 9, 25

E

Earth element, 11–12
Eclipses
  app for, 27
  impact of, 27–28
  lunar eclipse, 27–28
  recording, 37
  solar eclipse, 27–28
Elements, 11–12
Emotions
  moods and, 29, 35, 37–39, 41
  moon and, 23
  processing, 15, 37–38
  releasing, 38
  tracking, 35, 37–39, 41
Events, tracking, 40–185

F

Fire element, 11–12
Fixed quality, 11, 12
Forecasts, making, 6

G

Gemini, 11, 13–15

H

Horoscope
  app for, 40
  recording, 40-41,
    44-185
  sun signs and, 7, 40-41
  tracking, 7, 40-41
  website for, 40

J

Journal
  benefits of, 6-7, 9,
    37-41, 43
  birth chart for, 40
  daily information in,
    40-41
  explanation of, 36-37
  filling, 40-41
  horoscope for, 40-41
  mood details for, 41
  pages for, 42-185
  productive journaling, 39
  recording details in,
    40-41
  reflecting on, 40-41
  tips for, 6-7, 39-41
  tracking patterns in,
    6-7, 37-41
  using, 36-41
Journal pages, 42-185
Jupiter transits, 33

L

Leo, 11, 12, 16
Libra, 11, 12, 18
Lunar cycle
  app for, 29
  description of, 23-24
  impact of, 23-25
  moon phases, 23-25,
    29, 40
  tracking, 40
Lunar eclipse, 27-28

M

Mars retrograde, 31
Mercury retrograde,
  29-31, 34
Mindfulness, 31, 38
Moods, 29, 35, 37-39, 41
Moon phases
  app for, 29
  dark moon, 24
  decision-making and, 25
  description of, 23-25
  emotions and, 23
  full moon, 24
  impact of, 23-25
  lunar cycle, 23-25, 29,
    40
  new moon, 23-24
  recording, 37
  sun signs and, 23-24
  void-of-course moon, 25
  waning moon, 24

Mooncalendar.Astro-Seek
  .com, 29
Mutable quality, 12-13
My Moon Phase app, 29

N

Neptune transits, 34-35

P

Patterns
  cycles and, 6-7, 26
  formation of, 6
  tracking, 6-7, 37-41
  uncovering, 38
Personal growth, 28,
  37-38, 41, 43
Pisces, 11, 13, 22
Planetary cycles
  impact of, 29-35
  patterns and, 6-7
  recording, 37
  study of, 6-7
Planets
  cycles of, 6-7, 29-35, 37
  impact of, 11, 28-35
  Jupiter transits, 33
  Mars retrograde, 31
  Mercury retrograde,
    29-31, 34
  Neptune transits, 34-35
  Pluto transits, 34-35
  ruling planets, 11-21, 30
  Saturn return, 31-33

sun signs and, 29–35
Uranus transits, 34
Venus retrograde, 31
Pluto transits, 34–35
Predictions, making, 6

Q

Quadruplicities, 12–13
Qualities
    cardinal quality, 11, 12
    fixed quality, 11, 12
    mutable quality, 12–13

R

Reflections, 6–7, 35–38, 40–41
Resources, 186–87
Retrograde explanation, 29–30. *See also specific planets*

S

Sagittarius, 11, 13, 19–20
Saturn return, 31–33
Scorpio, 11, 12, 18–19
Seasonal cycles
    description of, 26
    patterns and, 6, 26
    study of, 6
    tracking, 37
Seasons
    changes and, 13, 26

description of, 26
fixed signs and, 12
patterns of, 6, 26
qualities and, 12–13
recording, 37
Self-care, 28, 33, 34, 39, 43
Solar cycle, 26
Solar eclipse, 27–28
Spiritual growth, 37–38, 41, 43
Stars, as guide, 6
Stars, power of, 9
Stress, relieving, 31, 37–38
Stress, triggering, 28, 34
Sun, impact of, 11, 26
Sun signs. *See also specific signs*
    birth chart and, 6–7, 11, 40
    elements and, 11–12
    horoscope and, 7, 40–41
    impact of, 11–22
    moon and, 23–24
    planets and, 29–35
    qualities and, 11–13

T

Taurus, 11, 12, 14
TimePassages app, 40
Triplicities, 11–12
Trismegistus, Hermes, 28

U

Uranus transits, 34

V

Venus retrograde, 31
Virgo, 11, 13, 17
Void-of-course (VoC) moon, 25. *See also Moon phases*

W

Water element, 11–12
Websites, 29, 40, 187
We'Moon Datebook, 28

Z

Zodiac signs, 11–24, 29–35. *See also specific signs*

About the Author

Mecca Woods is a New York City-based astrologer and author who works to help others create a life they truly want using their natural-born gifts. Her writing and astro-guidance have appeared in places like *Bustle* and *Essence*, as well as on TLC. She is also the author of *Astrology for Happiness and Success* and the Your Cosmic Coloring Book series. When she's not writing, Mecca is teaching astrology classes on personal development and cohosting the astrology podcast *Stars on Fire*. Her most important job is being a mom to her awesome Aries daughter. You can find Mecca at MyLifeCreated.com.

"The perfect star-inspired guide to life."
—Essence

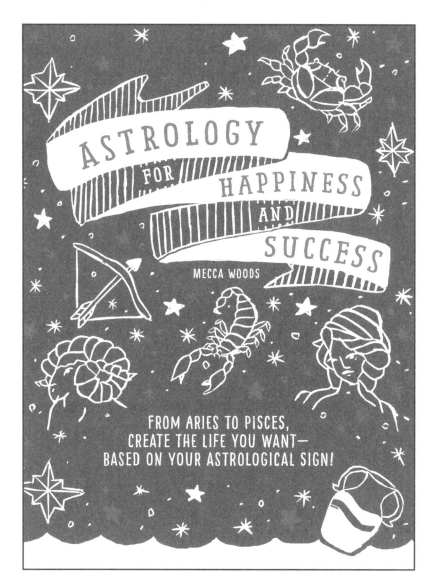